I0135945

NEW MEDIA AND THE CHRISTIAN FAMILY

EXPERIENCES FROM THE USA AND AFRICA

BY WILFRED EMEH

Foreword by
David Anders, PhD

New Media and the Christian Family:
Experiences from the USA and Africa

All rights reserved
Copyright © 2016 by Wilfred Epie Emeh

ISBN: 978-0-692-79516-3

No part of this publication may be reproduced, stored in a retrieval
system, or transmitted in any form or by any means electronic,
mechanical, photocopying, recording, or otherwise, without the
written permission of the author or publisher.

Printed in the United States by TransAmerica Printing,
Birmingham, Alabama
Distributed in the United States and Africa

To Bishop Pius S. Awa of Blessed Memory (1930-2014)

To African Families at home and abroad

*To the Parishioners, Our Lady of Sorrows Church,
Homewood, Alabama.*

TABLE OF CONTENTS

FOREWORD

Fr. Wilfred Emeh has written a fascinating account of the Christian Family in its encounter with the New Media. No one is more qualified to address these timely questions. Fr. Wilfred is a priest from Cameroon, West Africa with graduate and undergraduate degrees in communications, who has served parishes in the United States and Cameroon. His sociological studies have been supplemented by deep pastoral experience across cultures and family structures. He is no stranger to the challenges pressuring families across the globe. With hard science and colorful stories, he moves us with sometimes surprising accounts of sorrow and joy.

In his research and stories, Fr. Wilfred highlights those people who have been drawn away from family by cultural and economic forces. We meet the aged Americans left to die alone in nursing homes, an institution unknown in Cameroon. We meet the Cameroonian immigrants, working slavishly in the New World to provide for family members at home, unaware of how much their new life would cost them in time away from family life. We meet American and Cameroonian children, anxious to fit into the new entertainment culture, alienated from both their parents and their culture.

Undoubtedly, the entertainment culture has contributed to the breakdown of families. Electronic communication has the power to unite immigrant families separated by thousands of miles. It also has the power to draw children away from family bonds and into worlds with sometimes only tenuous connections to reality. Nowhere is this break from reality more visible or more damaging than in the assault on traditional family structure.

Some in the New Media treat traditional family as a fiction, an arbitrary ideal imposed by Western, Christian society. Nothing could be farther from the truth. As Fr. Emeh shows, commitment to an objective moral order governing marriage is universal, even apart from Western Christianity. The strength of family bonds in traditional Cameroon is testament to this fact.

For all the historical and cultural variations in marriage, children everywhere are born from a mother and a father. This is not just true for Christians. Cultures throughout history and across the globe have recognized that children have certain physical and moral needs. They need to be loved, educated, and nurtured. The people best equipped and most immediately responsible for those needs are the parents. Marriage is simply society's way of recognizing this objective moral order. This is why marriage, throughout history, is essentially connected to fecundity, to childbirth, and to the bonds of kindship established between those who bring new life into the world.

The Catholic Church recognizes this natural moral order and the good of natural marriage. Anytime a man and a woman (Christian or not) pledge themselves to one another for the sake of family, we can potentially have the good of marriage. But the Church also recognizes a higher form of marital union, the marriage of the baptized. Because baptism makes us members of Christ, the baptized couple brings Jesus into their marriage. His grace elevates this naturally good marriage into something supernaturally good. It becomes a sacrament. The light of that sacrament illumines every marriage, and shows how cultural variations in marriage may not always be ennobling. The preacher's task is to elevate *every* marriage to the idea of love established by Christ.

I know Fr. Wilfred as just such a preacher. In fact, he is an unusually talented priest. For the last few years, he has served at Our Lady of Sorrows Church in Homewood, Alabama, where my family belongs. He is highly regarded as one of the best preachers in our diocese, who can humorously relate his life in Cameroon to the real difficulties of American families. I have also encountered Fr. Wilfred the scholar, sharing research and discussion about the latest sociological data, drawing keen insight from his cross-cultural perspective. I also know Fr. Wilfred as a creative media missionary, seeking to make use of technology to spread the gospel across the globe.

It is with great pleasure that I recommend his book *New Media and the Christian Family: Experiences from the USA and Africa.* I read it with great interest and will use his insights in my own media apostolate. Working in Catholic radio, I am privileged to speak with families around the globe. I can assure you they all want authentic, spiritual lives, ennobled by truth, drawn together in love. Fr. Wilfred's book is a helpful tool for those seeking insight into family life in this new media environment.

David Anders, Ph.D.
Host of *Called to Communion*
EWTN Global Catholic Radio Network

ACKNOWLEDGMENTS

Many people contributed to the realization of this book. I am grateful to Professor Mark Hickson, III, whose outstanding lectures inspired me to work on this topic. I am equally thankful to Professor Larry Powell for his pertinent suggestions regarding my research methods. Many thanks to Professors Jonathan Amsbary, Virginia Richmond, Eduardo Neiva, and Hee Sun Park for their support.

Special words of appreciation go to my Pastor, Reverend Monsignor Martin Muller, and the staff and parishioners at Our Lady of Sorrows Church for their spiritual and moral support. I would like to acknowledge Jimmy and Nannette Baecher, John Tombrello, Jude Tombrello, Kent and MaryAnne Graeve, Philipp and Carol Rumore, James Lovell, Trudy Confessore, Daphne Carr, Ellen Shuman, Michael Tapley, Brent and Lacie Bilodeau, Gary and Laney Gagnon, Tricia and Jerry Kitchens, Paula and Ebb Berry, Gary and Carrie Khodanian, Heather and Richard Campbell, and Richard Atem.

Many thanks to my family and friends, who tirelessly support me in my ministry.

I am particularly grateful to Dr. David Anders for his thoughtful and inspiring foreword. Special words of thanks to Michelle Johnson for her moral and spiritual support.

Above all, I give praise and thanks to God Almighty for who I am and for all that I have been able to accomplish thus far in my priestly ministry. May His name be praised, now and forever!

INTRODUCTION

"Johnny Just Come"

It is every immigrant's fear that they—or worse, their children—will leave their home country and change for the worse because they are no longer connected with a culture that shares their values.

When I moved to the United States in 2013, I was pleased to find a home-away-from-home in the form of a thriving Cameroonian diaspora community located close to the college I was attending in Maryland. I was drawn to this community, not just by virtue of shared nationality, but, more importantly, by the celebration of mass on Sundays. Although my primary purpose for moving to the United States was to attend school, I ministered during my spare time, and I found it was a comfort to find my "family" in the Christian community. As a "Johnny just come,"[1] or JJC, it thrilled me to find such a large group of people from my home country with whom to interact. Still, I was in for a major dose of culture shock. Although ministering is integral to my calling, there were pastoral challenges, and life in general was very different from the experiences I had had in Cameroon.

I spent quite some time visiting hospices and nursing homes, where I ministered to the sick and elderly, many of whom were American-born Caucasians. Most of the individuals I had the honor of meeting in these facilities were people who truly required the care and compassion that the nurses and staff provided. In general, residential care offers people with mild health problems

---

1   A Nigerian slang term for a recent immigrant arrival, especially a naïve newcomer

a unique environment in which to live, offering residents the comfort of home as well as social community to stay active in.

Nevertheless, it was different from my experiences, and it took me time to adjust. After all, in Cameroon, the whole community comes together to celebrate and honor the elderly, taking care of them as though they were family, even if they are not related by blood. While many of the residents in these facilities were visited regularly by family, some of the men and women with whom I met were fortunate to see a family member once a year; others had no one left to care for them.

As I ministered to the sick and elderly, I took time to listen to their stories. Many of their lives were very different from the lives of the Cameroonian elders with whom I had spoken, and the differences concerned me. For many, their choices had led them to having limited family upon which to rely. Some had been married once, but decided not to have children. Others had one or two children who had preceded them in death. For some, their surviving family was either too far away or didn't care enough to visit. And some had never been married.

The experiences of these men and women were not the only ones that baffled me. As members of the diaspora know, homosexuality is illegal in Cameroon. Being openly homosexual can result in prison time and hefty fines, as well as a negative overall cultural judgment of those individuals. In America, however, homosexuals often are open about their sexualities and can even be married to same-sex partners in the eyes of the law. I had heard stories about this, of course, but it was a very new and strange thing to me when I ultimately met with a gay couple who were looking forward to adopting a little girl.

One thing I have learned in the U.S. is to sincerely respect all people, no matter what their beliefs or practices are, even when I feel embarrassed. It is not, after all, my place to judge them—only God can do that.[2] Jesus commands us:

---

2   James 4:12; Matthew 7:1-5; Luke 6:37

"Treat others as you would like people to treat you. If you love those who love you, what credit can you expect? Even sinners love those who love them. And if you do good to those who do good to you, what credit can you expect? For even sinners do that much…Be compassionate just as your Father is compassionate."[3]

My experiences as a new nonimmigrant are familiar to other Cameroonians living in the United States. Feelings of loneliness, isolation, and culture shock are common among newcomers to any culture. The cultural differences I faced really struck me when I heard an anecdote of a man who asked a priest to offer a mass for his deceased dog. I never understood why the man would want a mass for a dog until I saw how people in the United States take care of their pets. Pets, especially dogs and cats, are integral family members, with real names. In fact, pets are the only "children" that some people ever have! This is much different from what I was used to in Cameroon. In the United States, people believe that pet owners owe their pets a good life. Eventually, I came to agree.

Once, I visited a parish in the diocese of Joliet, in Illinois. The Pastor was away, but he told me where to pick up the keys and called my attention to his cat. I didn't sleep much because of the cat's meowing and yowling in front of the door all through the night. I felt sorry for the little cat because I had deprived her of her cozy room! This experience showed me that I was truly becoming integrated in my new country.

Despite our shared experiences as strangers in a strange land, many members of the Cameroonian diaspora can be quick to dismiss newcomers who express their dismay. I expressed my experiences with culture shock and my concerns over how family and marriage did not seem to be celebrated in my new country during one of my first homilies in Maryland. Yet, when I tried

3   Luke 6:31-33, 36

to engage the parishioners afterwards, most simply offered me a resigned, "Welcome to America."

One parishioner took the time to speak with me. "Father, you see, we just celebrated mass at 2:30pm. Didn't it surprise you? How often do you celebrate afternoon masses in Cameroon? Life here is different. We are hustling! Some of us work 'round the clock to make ends meet. We come here not just for Mass but also to express ourselves culturally. This is the only mass some of us get to attend, once a month. Many of us stay back for the reception not just for food and drink but to sing and dance as we do back home."

My parishioner friend continued. "We would love to hold close to our hearts what we can of our culture and values in this country, but that can be a challenge. The social, cultural, and economic changes we face are often drastic and enormous, and we all must survive. The financial pressures on some immigrant families are excessive, and most of us find ourselves either in the middle or lower income class despite taking on sometimes two or more full-time jobs—and sometimes, even that is not enough to make ends meet."

Raising Good Catholics, Good Cameroonians, and Good Americans

It is every parent's calling to raise their child in ways that are pleasing in the Lord's sight, and every parent struggles at times to fulfill this divine mandate. Children are a blessing, but they also offer parents new challenges with every day.

One of the biggest challenges Catholic parents, and Cameroonian parents in particular, face in America is the external influence of new media. The rise of social media and overall Internet use has created dramatic changes in communication in the new millennium. Electronic media now dominate the transmission of culture, and we spend more time than ever exploring, interacting with, and experiencing media. Today's media are the windows of our culture, since they provide the myths, the stories, and the images that help us explore who we are, what we can do, and what we can become.

The Church has called the Christian family the "Domestic Church" since antiquity. As such, matters that affect the Christian family also directly affect the Church. To maintain its relevance, the Church must consider the influence of media in the pastoral care of families.

New media often embraces non-Catholic values, and unfortunately, it plays a much bigger role in the way children grow to see the world than many of us would like. Media is a strong influencer of morality, and without guidance, Christian families may find their children's morals moving away from those of the Church due to media influence.

As I earlier indicated, cultural transition is never an easy experience. Acclimatizing was an uphill task for me, yet I sailed on with great delight because I was certain that someday I would find a bright light at the end of the tunnel. Of course, highs and lows, shocks and embarrassments, joys and sorrows were a part of my story. As I pondered everything, my thoughts settled on family—perhaps because of the vast differences I observed between the American and the African families. This led me to put together my thoughts on family dynamics within the two cultures. I administered a questionnaire to children in Cameroon and the United States to tap their understanding of marriage and family and the impact of the new media on traditional family values. Their answers were extremely revealing.

This book explores contemporary perceptions of family and marriage, mostly drawn and analyzed from the survey results. It looks into the relationship between the family dynamic and media influence. The media's influence can inform and encourage specific family values—or it can be used for the opposite purpose. Destructive messages and ideologies can spread just as easily as positive ones. Christian families in particular may find their values being represented less frequently, replaced with values they do not hold true.

There is no gainsaying the fact that as families navigate the new media while the Church tirelessly proclaims the family as the bedrock of society, there is urgent need to move in the right direction. It is the task of all parents to carefully balance their children's need to feel and act American with their African cultural heritage and their Catholic spirituality. There will always be some adjustment when moving to a place with a different culture. However, that does not mean that you or your children must discard your religious or cultural values, nor does it mean that you cannot exert your influence on American culture to more strongly reflect your values. This book offers practical guidelines to parents, teachers, youth ministers, and pastors on the most suitable ways to navigate the complicated waters of raising children with traditional Catholic values in a media saturated culture.

CHAPTER 1

Changing Views of Traditional Marriage

A Bishop was quizzing children before their Confirmation. He came to one nervous little girl and asked, "What is matrimony?"

She answered, "Matrimony is the place where souls suffer for a time for their sins."

"No, no," said the parish priest, "that is purgatory."

The Bishop replied, "What do you and I know about it? She might be right!"

This joke speaks volumes about the reality of marriages today. While the little girl was simply mistaken, ask around, and you will find someone who truly believes that marriage is a form of purgatory—or worse. Conventional wisdom holds that it is not uncommon for marriages to struggle from time to time; however, the belief that marriage only brings suffering is becoming all too common in cultures around the world.

God never intended marriage to be a form of purgatory. In fact, He in His wisdom made marriage one of the most beautiful gifts to humanity. Marriage may be seventh on the list of sacraments, but it is certainly not the least! After all, it is only through the sacrament of marriage that couples should bring children into the world.

Marriage, according to the Code of Canon Law, section 1, "is the matrimonial covenant, by which a man and a woman establish between themselves a partnership of the whole of life and which is ordered by its nature to the good of the spouses and the procreation and education of offspring, has been raised by Christ the Lord to the dignity of a sacrament between the baptized."[4] Christians have children not merely to continue the species and build up society but so that the whole family might be formed for the communion of saints.

Catholic marriage is the starting point of a new family's life. When a man and a woman marry by freely consenting to mutual promises of fidelity and permanence, marriage places procreation in the context of human dignity and freedom. The marital vows are analogous to God's covenant with Israel and the Church.[5]

As John Paul II points out, "From the wedlock of Christians, there comes the family, in which new citizens of human society are born, who by the grace of the Holy Spirit received in baptism are made children of God, thus perpetuating the people of God through the centuries. When they become parents, spouses receive from God the gift of a new responsibility. Their children see the love their parents offer as the visible sign of the very love of God, 'from whom every family in heaven and on earth is named.'"[6]

Media and Marriage

The world is changing, and with it, views on traditional Catholic values are changing. Children are especially vulnerable, and children of the diaspora are even more vulnerable than those still living within their native land. In spite of their parents' best efforts, Catholic children are becoming increasingly accepting of non-Catholic views on marriage, including divorce, remarriage after divorce, same-sex marriage, remaining unmarried, and even having sexual relations outside the bonds of marriage.

This acceptance is directly in conflict with the teachings of the Church, which state that marriage is a lifelong covenant between

---

4   Code of Canon Law, c 1055, §1
5   A Preparatory Catechesis for the World Meeting of Families, 2015
6   John Paul II, 1981

a man, a woman, and God. There are myriad reasons for children accepting these non-Catholic values, with the consumption of new media being one of the most notable.

Now, this is not to say that all media consumption is bad or will encourage your children to stray from their traditional Catholic values. Catholic and Christian family-friendly media content is still being produced and distributed in both the U.S. and Cameroon. However, that content is an increasingly small percentage of the content to which Catholic children are exposed.

There can be no question that media in the modern age has changed dramatically from its early origins. Even within the last half of the 20th century, the changes in content and quality are staggering. As one parent put it in an interview,

> "I think [media is] hugely different from when I was a kid. When I was a kid, the shows were, there was hardly any violence on the shows. A lot of family-related shows, that's what we saw all the time. I mean even things like *Bonanza*, where there were people getting shot once in a while, it wasn't this continual blood and you never saw anything, it wasn't just people going after each other with machine guns."[7]

Violence, sexual content, and drug use are almost commonplace in media these days. The representation of marriage in the media has also changed. While we no longer have Ralph Kramden of *The Honeymooners* threatening spousal abuse for laughs, we also no longer have an overwhelming majority of married couples who portray the virtues of a traditional Catholic marriage. While iconic couples like Rob and Laura Petrie of *The Dick Van Dyke Show*, Lucy and Ricky Ricardo of *I Love Lucy*, and June and Ward Cleaver of *Leave It to Beaver* may not have been explicitly Catholic in their shows, they offer working examples of traditional marriages with the goals of staying together for life and creating families with strong Christian values.

---

7   Hoover, Clark, and Alters, 2004, p. 62

Traditional Catholic marriages, specifically heterosexual couples who stay together for life, have become less and less commonplace in modern American media. The holy sacrament of marriage is cast aside to showcase interpretations of what "family" means in America today—and those interpretations all too often fly in the face of Catholicism's teachings on the sacrament. Take the popular "family" show, *Modern Family*, which regularly draws in over 11.5 million viewers with each episode and which has won an embarrassing number of awards.[8] As its name suggest, the show offers viewers a glimpse into the lives of five interrelated "modern families." Yet, of these five families, none of them offer viewers the values of a traditional Catholic marriage. Two couples (Jay and DeDe; Gloria and Javier) are divorced. Gloria and Jay married each other after their respective divorces. Mitch and Cam have a same-sex marriage. Even the enduring 20-year marriage between Claire and Phil Dunphy began due to a pregnancy, which was the result of their engaging in premarital sex.

Modern Family is just one example plucked from thousands. Indeed, it's far more difficult to find an example of a show that does teach traditional Catholic values (and stick to those values throughout its run) than to find a show like *Modern Family*.

Members of the Cameroonian diaspora can find themselves feeling particularly vulnerable to media influence. There is an extreme societal pressure to conform to American morality and cultural norms. Parents who are confident in their cultural and moral identity are able to stand strong against these tides, but children and teens, who lack that confidence, are filled with a desire to "fit in" and be "more American." They worry that if they do not watch the right shows, listen to the right music, or join the right social media networks, that they will be seen even more

---

8   As of April 1, 2016, Modern Family had won: 21 Emmy Awards, 6 Writers Guild of America Awards, 5 Screen Actors Guild Awards, 4 Producers Guild of America Awards, 3 Television Critics Awards, 2 Art Directors Guild Awards, 2 Directors Guild Awards, 2 GLAAD Media Awards, 2 NAACP Image Awards, 2 Nickelodeon Kids' Choice Awards, 1 Golden Globe Award, 1 Peabody Award, and 1 Young Artist Award.

4

as outsiders than they already are—a terrifying prospect for any young person.

That societal pressure combined with consumption of new media manifests itself in generational loss of Catholic values. Traditional Catholic values are, at times, in conflict with American society, which by and large accepts non-traditional "marriages" (including divorce, remarriage, same-sex marriages, and even unmarried couples living together in sin), embraces artificial means of birth control and abortion, and elevates material worth over spiritual and moral value.

Media in America represents a wide variety of viewpoints, including those which are not Catholic or even Christian. This diversity can be a wonderful thing, as it offers new perspectives and it ensures that many people, including Catholics, can have a voice. However, it also allows for the creation of media that does not reflect Catholic values. Over time, non-Catholic media has grown increasingly accepting of values that directly clash with Catholicism's teachings, placing vulnerable Catholic children in the crosshairs of a moral conflict.

CHAPTER 2

Access to New Media

In the 21st century America, new media is almost impossible to escape. Nearly everyone has instant access to the whole world of media through their phones and computers. Every bit of media is digital and can be downloaded for either free or a small charge. Even if your family decides to live television- and computer-free in your home (which is becoming increasingly impossible to do), many churches, schools, libraries, and other public spaces offer access to media for free.

Media Access in the USA

As of 2015[9], an astonishing 84% of American adults used the Internet. The usage rate differs by age: only 58% of American senior citizens (age 65+) used the Internet, whereas 93% of adults 18-29 used the Internet. Usage is far more widespread among younger adults and youths, who grew up or are growing up in a world where Internet use was and is widespread.

American children and teenagers are growing up in a world that expects them to have access to media and to take advantage of that access by going online, watching television, and so forth. These expectations are not unreasonable given the level of media saturation in children's lives. According to a 2015 Pew Research Center report[10]:

---

9   Perrin & Duggan, 2015
10   Lenhart, 2015

- Nearly a quarter (24%) of teens report going online "almost constantly," thanks in part to their access to smartphones. A whopping 92% of teens go online at least once daily.

- An enormous 71% of teens use more than one social networking site, with Facebook being the most popular. The average teenager uses these sites to connect with hundreds of accounts. These accounts can belong to personal friends and family, or to businesses, celebrities, and political groups. Some connections may be total strangers.

- Among American teens, 88% have access to a mobile phone, while 73% of teens have smartphones. The increase in smartphone use among teenagers has drastically increased their exposure to new media and total time spent online.

- The average teenager experiences an impressive amount of virtual communication.

- Ninety percent of teens who have access to cell phones will exchange texts. American teens send and receive an average of 30 texts per day. In addition to texts, 33% of teens use separate messaging apps, like Kik, WhatsApp, Facebook Messenger, and Snapchat to communicate virtually.

- The statistics for tablets and computer access are also very high. 87% of American teens have access to a laptop or desktop computer, and 58% have access to a tablet.

With this nearly ubiquitous media availability, is it any wonder that the American teenager is known best for hiding in their media-rich bedroom with a "Parents: Keep Out!" sign on the door?[11] In Cameroon, the same children would be out playing with their friends or would choose to spend quality time with their family—possibly because personalized media access is not as available.

Media Access in Cameroon

The widespread media availability we find in the U.S is very different from what we have in Cameroon. While there are hundreds of television channels available via cable and satellite in the U.S, there are fewer channels available on satellite and dozens of others via cable in different regions of the country.[12] Likewise, there are fewer radio stations and newspapers. "Cameroon Web" lists a total of 67 radio stations in seven regions of the country, along with about 14 regularly published newspapers and many others that rise and fall. Most of these stations are not officially licensed, and, with improper management, they rarely survive the test of time and capitalism.[13] Unlicensed ham radio operators help to bolster the availability of expression and media, but they are subject to being shut down at any time if they are perceived to have crossed a line.[14]

Data from Internet world stats indicate that 11% of Cameroonians (2.6 million of a population of 23.7 million people) use the Internet, and 1.4 million of these are active on Facebook. RANSBIZ has rated Facebook as the most popular social networking site in Cameroon, followed by Twitter. The Friedrich Ebert Foundation, however, in 2014 published a report that ranked LinkedIn as the second most used networking site.

As it stands, social media is popular among the roughly 5% of the Cameroonian population who currently access the Internet. Facebook is the 5th most popular website visited,[15] and Twitter is

---

11   Livingstone & Bovill, 2001
12   BBC News, 2015
13   Halle, 2013
14   Central Intelligence Agency, 2016
15   Internet World Stats, 2014

so popular that the government shut it down within the country in 2011, when citizens planned demonstrations against long-standing President Biya.

Seventy-five in every 100 Cameroonians have a cell phone, which will eventually allow for greater Internet saturation. However, at this time, the cell infrastructure is stuck in the 3G era at its best.[16] Delays have slowed the launch of 3G in some areas, but there is hope that 4G availability will be widespread by 2017 or 2018. 4G access will allow more Cameroonians to access the Internet through their cell phones, bolstering Internet use throughout the country.

Transitioning from Media in Cameroon to Media in the U.S.

In terms of media alone, there is a stark difference between life in Cameroon and life in the U.S. Adjusting to media's omni-presence and the variety of media available in the U.S. can be a huge challenge for members of the Cameroonian diaspora.

Within the U.S., media and technology have become paramount in the lives of children and young adults. Parents must find a way to capitalize on the benefits of media while facing the many challenges presented by constant and instant access to new media.

Parents' Responsibility

Americans place great value on encouraging students to learn how to use and consume media, and many American schools incorporate learning media technologies into classes for students starting at a very young age. Although children will be exposed to media through their schools, daycares, and public places, parents play a large role in a child's ability to access media. Parents are typically the first and primary providers of the tools and the knowledge that allow children to access media.

This responsibility can feel overwhelming, and many parents are unsure of how to navigate it. Some parents respond to this responsibility by denying their children access to media. This

---

16 Lancaster, 2015

response, however, is unrealistic because of the public availability of media. There also is a social agreement in the U.S. that students must learn how to use media within schools. Unless you decide to never let your children leave your home, it is inevitable that they will encounter media in some form or another.

Other parents go the opposite direction and adopt a very laissez-faire attitude towards their children's media consumption. While this certainly is an easy path to take, it exposes children to media that may conflict with the Catholic values and upbringing their parents are attempting to instill.

Catholic parents need to seek out a happy medium between these two extremes of media use. You can teach your child responsible ways to use and engage in media without cutting them off from media entirely. Chapter 8 has an in-depth how-to guide for finding this balance within your family.

As St. John Paul II so wisely noted in his Redemptoris Missio[17]:

> "The first Areopagus[18] of the modern age is the world of communications, which is unifying humanity and turning it into what is known as a 'global village.' The means of social communication have become so important as to be for many the chief means of information and education, of guidance and inspiration in their behavior as individuals, families and within society at large."

Media is crucial to both modern American life and modern evangelism. Like all things in this world, the new media is a gift from God—however, like all gifts from God, it is up to us to use it wisely.

---

17   John Paul II, 1990
18   Important tribunal

CHAPTER 3

Benefits and Detriments of Media Use

The media revolution prompted innumerable changes in offices and classrooms across the globe; however, the most notable changes occurred on a personal level, affecting the way individuals and families communicated with each other and the world. Thanks to advances in computer technology, computers transformed from bulky machines sized exclusively for corporate offices and government buildings into smaller personal devices that could easily fit into people's homes, cars, and even purses or pockets.

Nearly every household in the United States now has access to a personal computer, not counting computer availability at work, school, and local libraries. According to the most recent Census Bureau's estimates,[19] 83.8% of all American households own a computer, with 74.4% having some form of Internet access at home. This explosion of accessibility has deeply enriched social connection and education, while simultaneously presenting a new set of challenges for the family.

In his message on the 38th World Communication Day, Pope John Paul II noted:

> "The extraordinary growth of the communications media and their increased availability has brought exceptional opportunities for enriching the lives not only of individuals, but also of families. At the same time, families today face new

---

19   File & Ryan, 2014

challenges arising from the varied and often contradictory messages presented by the mass media. The theme chosen for the 2004 World Communications Day 'The Media and the Family: A Risk and a Richness' is a timely one, for it invites sober reflection on the use which families make of the media and, in turn, on the way that families and family concerns are treated by the media."[20]

The sainted Pope's message is as relevant today as it was then. The accessibility of communications media has improved the lives of numerous individuals and families, while simultaneously creating challenges, especially regarding content, overuse, and misuse. It is vital to recognize and respond to these challenges in order to create a healthy media environment in your home.

Media Content: Advertising, Violence, and Sexuality

As media consumers, we have the least amount of control over the content that is produced. In fact, unless you work in the mass communications industry, you have almost no control over what is available on television, radio, and the Internet. While on-demand streaming services like Netflix, Hulu, and Amazon Prime, and DVR systems have made it easier for you and your family to choose specific content to watch at any given time, these services do still offer programming that opposes Catholic values.

It is crucial that you take control of the content in your home, especially in the areas of advertising, violence, and sexual content. If you have ever noticed how enthralled children become with certain shows, singing along, mimicking dances, counting, and even responding to onscreen questions, you understand why it is so important to be responsible about what content enters your home.

Children are miniature sponges absorbing media content without discrimination, whether it is good or bad, fiction or reality, programming or commercials. An article in *Psychology Today* points out that younger children cannot differentiate be-

---

20   John Paul II, 2004

tween commercials and actual programming, and they are less likely to know the difference between fiction and reality.[21] This can be dangerous for the viewer if the content is sending inappropriate messages or mixed moral views. Repeated exposure to media messages could shape a viewer's perception of reality. Those who spend more time 'living' in the world of television are more likely to see the 'real world' in terms of the images, values, portrayals, and ideologies that emerge through the lens of the television.[22]

What does this mean for your child and their sponge-like brain? The media is shaping, molding, and educating them on a daily basis through scenes and images, dialogue, body language, and additional information. The morals, lifestyles, and decisions expressed in the media will make an impression on your child, whether for good or bad. There is no better reason for monitoring what your children listen to, watch, and read in the digital world, as children are particularly prone to media's effects.

Advertising and the Child Consumer

The average child views a reported 40,000 commercials per year.[23] It is no surprise that recent studies have revealed that young children can recognize logos and the status associated with certain brand names at a very young age. During a small study of 38 Australian preschoolers, researchers Anna McAllister and T. Bettina Cornwell discovered that, "Children as young as three are feeling social pressure and understand that consumption of certain brands can help them through life."[24] In the same study, 93% of the preschoolers recognized fast food brands targeted at their age group. The researchers caution, "Findings like this show us that we need to think about materialism developing in very young children," and that, "we also need to realize that it's not completely 'safe' to leave a 3-year-old

---

21   Vitelli, 2013
22   Morgan, Shanahan, & Signorielli, 2009
23   Vitelli, 2013
24   as cited in Bryner, 2010

alone with a TV set without proper supervision or a parent to help them to understand that they are on the receiving end of targeted advertising."[25] Advertisers entice children to want the toys, food, snacks, and clothes in their commercials through visual images and graphics designed specifically to draw young viewers in. Repeated and unmonitored exposure to colorful ads and commercials can encourage materialism and jealousy at a very young age, and if left unchecked can take root, leading to future materialistic behavior.

In one extreme case, advertising-driven materialism led a teen to commit murder. In the early 1990s, seventeen-year-old Demetrick James Walker was sentenced to life in prison for killing a sixteen-year-old boy for his $125 Nike AirJordans. Demetrick wanted the shoes he had seen advertised on TV so badly that he murdered another child to get them. During the trial, Houston prosecutor Mark Vinson placed some of the blame on the images created by advertising: "It's bad when we create an image of luxury about athletic gear that it forces people to kill over it."[26]

While advertising is not entirely to blame for this crime, there is no doubt that the developing minds of children and teens are highly susceptible to advertising messages. There is a reason why the Master Settlement Agreement banned tobacco companies from targeting youth in 1998, and no alcohol or tobacco ads are allowed within 500 feet of a school—children and young adults absorb and act on messages in advertising. Any parent who has survived the toy catalogs, relentless commercials, and general consumerism at Christmastime knows the power advertising has on children and adolescents. In order to prevent materialism, jealousy, and consumerism from taking root in your home, you must monitor and limit your family's exposure to advertising messages.

25   as cited in Bryner, 2010
26   Colford, Magiera, & Sloan, 1990

Violence and Aggression in Children

Ads are not the only media content negatively affecting children. Exposure to violence through media can have damaging effects on adolescents—especially minorities, emotionally disturbed and abused children, children with learning disabilities, and those children in families experiencing distress in the home. This is no surprise based on the sheer number of violent acts seen by children while watching television. "The average child sees 12,000 violent acts on television annually, including many depictions of murder and rape."[27] That translates to roughly 230 violent acts per week, or 33 acts of violence per day. Those numbers do not account for exposure to violent song lyrics or video games, where more than 90% of games rated appropriate for children 10 years or older contain violence.[28]

These numbers are distressing when one understands how the mind of a child works in relation to imitation and communication. The British psychologist, professor, and founder of the British Infancy Research Group, George Butterworth, says it best: "Modern research has shown imitation to be a natural mechanism of learning and communication which deserves to be at center stage in developmental psychology."[29]

A fundamental part of a child's cognitive development is communication through imitation. Every parent knows that children will imitate you, their friends, and their heroes in word and deed. It follows, then, that children who are repeatedly exposed to violent images and scenes through various forms of media may eventually imitate what they have seen in various degrees of severity.

There are those who would argue that the above statistics prove that children are exposed to significant amounts of violence, but that this exposure does not incite aggression in their behavior, or that imitation, if it happens at all, is too mild to fuss

---

27   Impact, 2003
28   Harvard, 2010
29   Butterworth & Nadel, 1999

17

over. However, studies performed in the United States would disagree. A family of researchers and professors, including Dr. Glenn Sparks, Dr. Cheri Sparks, and Erin Sparks, a Ph.D. candidate in Social Psychology, collaboratively researched and wrote an article concerning the causal relationship between media violence and aggression in children. Their conclusion:

> "Research on violent television and films, video games and music reveals unequivocal evidence that media violence increases the likelihood of aggressive and violent behavior in both immediate and long-term contexts. The effects appear larger for milder than for more severe forms of aggression, but the effects on severe forms of violence are also substantial… when compared with effects of other violent risks factors or medical effects deemed important by the medical community (e.g. aspirin on heart attacks)…the evidence is clearest with the most extensively researched domain, television and film violence."[30]

The American Academy of Pediatrics fully supports the Sparks' research results. The Academy States:

> "Research has associated exposure to media violence with a variety of physical and mental health problems for children and adolescents, including aggressive behavior, desensitization to violence, fear, depression, nightmares, and sleep disturbances. More than 3500 research studies have examined the association between media violence and violent behavior; all but 18 have shown a positive relationship."[31]

Nearly every single scientific study concerning media violence and aggressive behavior has shown a causal relationship. While it is unlikely that media violence would turn an other-

---

30   as cited in Bryant & Oliver, 2009
31   Committee on Public Education, 2001

wise fine child into a violent criminal, it certainly increases the probability of future violent behavior, just as every cigarette one smokes increases the likelihood of a lung tumor.[32] The evidence is undeniable. It is not a matter of *if* a child will react to violence on television and video games but *when*. Parents must be vigilant about limiting and eliminating violent media in their homes, especially for younger children.

Love, Marriage, and Sex

By now, you see the pattern—children absorb what they watch on television, listen to on the radio, and play on video games. The same holds true for the messages about love, marriage, and sex in the media. Take a look at these numbers:

- Today, sexual relations between unmarried individuals are shown 24 times more often than sex between spouses was in 1986.[33] Sexual content, married and unmarried, currently appears in 64% of all television programs. Programs with sexual content average 4.4 scenes with sexually related material per hour. Approximately 1 of every 7 programs (14%) includes a portrayal of sexual intercourse, depicted or strongly implied.[34]

- Teens rank the media as their primary source of information about sex, second to health class.[35]

- Kids with higher exposure to sex on television are almost twice as likely as kids with lower exposure to initiate sexual intercourse.[36]

32 Huesmann & Taylor, 2006
33 Greenberg & Hofschire, 2000
34 Farrar et al., 2003
35 American, 2001
36 Collins et al., 2004

- A survey of nearly 400 married individuals, analyzing television-viewing habits and related beliefs about marriage, relationships, and on-screen depictions of relationships, indicated that respondents who believe television relationships depict reality are more likely to cheat and less likely to stay in the marriage.[37]

It is no coincidence that children who regularly witness sexual scenes and images on television are two times more likely to initiate sex than kids with a lower exposure rate. They are imitating the messages they are most consistently receiving, and these messages no longer represent traditional family values.

In the 1950s, television shows depicted nuclear families with staunch morals, like *Leave it to Beaver*, *Father Knows Best*, and other examples we discussed previously. Television soon moved on to blended families, but still portrayed traditional values, as seen on *The Brady Bunch*. However, by the early '90s, programs like *Married with Children* and *Roseanne* exposed, and even promoted, family dysfunction and disrespect towards parental authority, sexuality, and alcohol. Since the millennium, the idea of a permanent marriage vow between a man and a woman is almost non-existent on television. Today, programming like *Desperate Housewives* and *Modern Family* define a new set of family values, while shows like *Sex and the City* send the message, "Why bother with marriage at all?" Even television programs marketed towards younger audiences, like *Gossip Girl*, *Glee*, and *Faking It*, promote serial dating, promiscuity, same-sex relationships, and a party lifestyle.

These alarming trends in television programming support what John Paul II meant when he stated:

> "The family and family life are all too often inadequately portrayed in the media. Infidelity, sexual activity outside of marriage, and the absence of a moral and spiritual vision of

---

37   Rozenfield, 2013

the marriage covenant are depicted uncritically, while positive support is at times given to divorce, contraception, abortion, and homosexuality. Such portrayals, by promoting causes inimical to marriage and the family, are detrimental to the common good of society."[38]

As parents, you must always remember that the media is in a conversation with your children. If the conversation consistently and repeatedly focuses on material goods, violence, pre-marital sex, and other non-Catholic behavior, your children are more likely to adopt, or worse, imitate these views.

Media Overuse

Even when parents are not struggling to control the content streaming through their homes, they are struggling to control the amount of time spent on media, good or bad. Nearly one-fourth, 24% to be exact, of all teens report going online "almost constantly."[39] Another study notes that 35% of the children live in homes where a television is on "always" or "most of the time."[40] Based on the minute-by-minute use of media, it is not an overstatement to say that the iPhone, the tablet, and so on, have all become more intimate companions to the users than fellow living humans beings.

How have the very devices designed to connect us to the outside world and each other managed to disconnect us? The simple answer is overuse. Children now have television sets in their bedrooms, personal computers in their family rooms, and cell phones in their backpacks. They spend more time engaging with media than doing any single activity other than sleeping. The average child consumes more than seven and half hours of media each day, not including media use at school, or time spent

38   John Paul II, 2004
39   Lenhart, 2015
40   Vandewater et al., 2005

using cell phones.[41] This is slightly under one-third of their entire day, and it's a huge chunk of their waking hours.

This overuse of media can result in a serious lack of personal social interaction, undermining the divine purpose for which God created man. It is evident in Sacred Scripture that man is a relational being, in need of social interaction and love. In the second chapter of Genesis, God created the animals because it was not good for man to be alone in the world. When these creatures did not suffice, God created woman, so that man would have a true partner.[42] By our very design, we need to be in relationships with other human beings. Ironically, modern communication technology, created to enhance communication between people, often prevents us from fulfilling our intended purpose—to be in relationships with God and others.

Perhaps the reason for this isolation is the advent of media-centered bedrooms, wherein children have private access to televisions, computers, and stereo equipment. In 2000, two-thirds of young children had a television in their bedroom, and 15% received cable channels in their bedrooms.[43] Almost all (96%) of the 8 through 18 year olds had some kind of audio system in their bedroom. Why would a child, especially a teenager who is asserting their independence, want to leave a room where they have uninterrupted access to their own music, movies, and social media?

The above scenarios and statistics have a negative impact on the family. Not only do children from media-oriented families read less,[44] they also spend more time watching media. One study of children from birth to age six reports that those who have a television set in their bedroom watch fifteen minutes more each day, and another study places the associated increase at thirty minutes. The difference in viewing time triples among eight- to eighteen-year-olds; those with no TV in their room report 2:04

---

41   Rideout, Foehr, & Roberts, 2010
42   Genesis 2:18-25
43   Roberts, 2000
44   Vandewater et al., 2005

hours of daily viewing time, while those with a TV claim 3:31 hours of daily viewing. The increase in viewing time vastly increases the number of media messages your child receives, while inversely decreasing the amount of time spent socializing with family and friends, studying, or participating in activities outside the home.

The proliferation of personal media within the context of the family, and their privatization, are a cause for concern. One study found that many adolescents are exposed to media with very limited or no parental control.[45] The researcher compared the number of adolescents who view television alone, with parents, or with siblings or peers. The results revealed that about one-fifth of 8 to 13 year-olds and one-third of 14 to 18-year-olds claimed that their overall daily television viewing occurred while they were mainly alone. The study included 487 media diaries from adolescents who recorded their television watching habits. These diaries indicate that preteens (8 to 13) spend 30% of their total television viewing time alone, while teenagers (14 to 18) spend 41% of their viewing time alone. Even more striking, only 6% of preteens and a mere 2% of teens watch television with a parent.

Parents are almost completely absent from the single most important, or at least, most prevalent, activity in their life—media time. Children are in an intense, and often unhealthy, relationship with media. If your adolescent son or daughter were to spend more than seven hours a day with a single person, who was consistently sending mixed and often immoral messages to your child, would you allow them to continue a relationship at that level? Of course not! There would be dire social and moral consequences to that type of codependence. It is essential that you see your child's interaction with media as a relationship. Like all healthy relationships, interaction with media demands limitations and boundaries.

---

45   Roberts, 2000

Media Misuse

No matter how positive your view or experience of media with your children may have been, there is always the possibility that they could suffer from misusing media themselves or that someone could victimize them through the media. Children and teens with unfettered access to media, especially the Internet, can be susceptible to a variety of media-related addictions, including addictions to pornography, gaming, and overall usage. They are also more likely to experience, witness, or take part in online bullying through social media, chat rooms, and anonymous blogging or posting. Unmonitored children can also stumble upon and fall prey to online predators. The opportunities for misuse are vast and should not be taken lightly.

Pornography and Addiction

Data from the Youth Internet Safety Survey revealed that the prevalence of seeing unwanted pornography increased from 25 percent in 2000, to 34 percent in 2005, and decreased to 23 percent in 2015.[46] This means roughly one-quarter to one-third of all teenagers who access the Internet are seeing unwanted pornographic images. These numbers do not include those teenagers who are intentionally searching for pornography online. The age of first exposure to pornography is now around 11 or 12.[47] Those numbers are distressing enough to any parent, and the idea that exposure to pornography might encourage your child to seek it out—or worse, become addicted to it—only adds to the urgency of careful Internet monitoring and the addition of blocking software.

Cyberbullying

The National Center for Education Statistics and Bureau of Justice Statistics from 2010–2011 revealed that 9% of students in grades 6–12 experienced cyberbullying. A separate survey

---

46   as cited in Israelsen-Hartley, 2014
47   Israelsen-Hartley, 2014

indicated that 15% of high school students were electronically bullied in 2013. These may seem like low numbers, but they are on the rise. Cyberbullying is a fairly new problem, and therefore lacks years of research, but its effects are clear. Children who are cyberbullied are more likely to do the following:

- Experiment with drugs and alcohol

- Skip school and make poor grades

- Have lower self-esteem and more health problems

- Experience anxiety and depression

Everyone experiences conflict during adolescence, but true cyberbullying is more than playground teasing, offensive comments, or simply not getting along with certain individuals. Bullying is repetitive in nature and can be verbal, physical, or social. There are serious consequences for both the victim and the aggressor that can last into adulthood. Cyberbullying allows the aggressor to threaten, insult, and harass their victim online, meaning their bullying follows your child throughout their day, even when they are in the assumed safety of your home. It is important to discuss the virtuous and kind use of texting and social media with your children, as well as how to handle any cyberbullying they may experience.

Predators

As parents, online sexual exploitation is the single most important Internet issue you can discuss with your children. Predators, pedophiles, and ill-intentioned adults regularly visit online forums created for children and teens, and they intend to cause mental, spiritual, and physical harm. Some seek online encounters through private or public chat rooms, while others aim to meet your child in person. According to the FBI, more than half a million pedophiles are online every day.[48]

These predators are master manipulators. They will stalk, trick, and manipulate their prey—your child—trying to groom them as their next victim. Online predators often create fake profiles, posing as teenagers. They try to connect with adolescents who have low self-esteem, parental struggles, and money shortages.

The prevalent use of social media among teens makes it fairly easy for predators to find their targets. Teenagers often post personal information, rants, and pictures on social media. Teenagers are also likely to friend or connect with strangers online. A veteran cyber investigator for the Chicago FBI offices commented that, in his experience, "about 70 percent of youngsters will accept 'friend' requests regardless of whether they know the requester."[49] These "friends" can then access any information your child puts on social media, including addresses, phone numbers, birthdays, interests, and photographs. Another FBI investigator warns, "Parents need to talk to their children about these issues. It's no longer enough to keep computers in an open area of the house so they can be monitored. The same thing needs to be done with online gaming platforms."[50] By creating clear boundaries and discussing online predators, you can help your children to make smart choices online and avoid people who may want to harm them. When it comes to your child's safety, it is always better to be overcautious. The risk simply isn't worth it.

Benefits of New Media in the Home

After reading about the dangers new media can present to your family, it may be hard to believe there is any good that can come of inviting new media into your home. However, just as there is evil in the world, there is also good. Media use is not

---

48   Federal Bureau of Investigation, 2011
49   Federal Bureau of Investigation, 2011
50   Federal Bureau of Investigation, 2011

without risks and flaws, but it also offers rewards and benefits. Family connection, education, and social communication can all benefit from informed and careful media use.

It should be noted here that there are no known benefits for children under the age of two in regards to media. In fact, the American Academy of Pediatrics recommends that children under two avoid screen time all together.[51] The new media benefits you will find here only apply to children ages three and up.

Family Connection

According to the survey by the Pew Internet and American Life Project, 42% of parents with a child ages 7 to 17 used their cell phone to call their child at least once a day.[52] More importantly, this survey found that 28% of families who owned cell phones and had access to the Internet reported that the use of such technology had brought their family closer together. Similar studies find that the use of social networking sites, such as Facebook, can help college students and deployed military personnel communicate with family members back home.[53] As we have become a busier and more mobile society, it is common for family members to be in several different places over the course of a day, and certainly over the course of a lifetime. Mobile devices and Internet capability have provided a wonderful communication platform for families to check in with younger children, stay in touch with college-aged kids, and e-mail or video chat with extended family across states, countries, and time zones. It is especially helpful for military families, and those families with jobs requiring extensive travel and relocation.

Additionally, cell phone use between family members has also been associated with greater family connection, parental knowledge, and parental peace of mind.[54] Today, children are more active outside the home, participating in clubs, service

51 American Academy of Pediatrics, 2013
52 Kennedy, Smith, Wells, & Wellman, 2008
53 Madge, Meek, Wellens, & Hooley, 2009; Schachman, 2010
54 as cited in Padilla-Walker, Coyne, & Fraser, 2012

organizations, sports, and the arts. Cell phones provide parents with the opportunity to monitor their child's social time with friends and family by allowing instant communication via text and the ability to locate a phone and its user using GPS.

Education

In addition to providing a means of communication, new media can also serve as a fine learning tool for preschoolers and elementary-aged children. When programs are designed to meet a young child's educational needs, they can stimulate gross motor skills and intellectual engagement. Additionally, well-designed educational programs, such as Sesame Street,[55] can teach four to five-year-olds basic reading and counting skills. Children in the same age group also benefit from pro-social messages on TV that encourage kindness and sharing. Beyond television programming, well-chosen apps and websites can assist with fine motor skills, gross motor functions, early literacy and numeracy proficiencies, and social abilities.

For older children, well-chosen video games and apps can encourage critical thinking skills, hand-eye coordination, problem-solving skills, and increased creativity. One Australian survey found that 94% of parents believe video games improved motor skills and hand-eye coordination in their children, while 91% believed video games assisted with problem-solving skills, and 72% felt that video games fostered creativity.[56] Additionally, apps and software can inspire creative thinking, and instill a love for art and music in young learners.

Pre-teens and teenagers can also benefit from new media in the home. In fact, many, if not all, schools require homework involving Internet research, the use of web-based teaching platforms, and multiple educational apps, all of which aim to pre-

---

55   As mentioned previously, even beneficial shows like *Sesame Street* can at times promote non-Catholic values, such as being accepting of divorce.
56   Raising Children Network, 2015

pare students for the future, increase engagement, and inspire technological collaboration.

Social Communication

One of the most obvious benefits of media in the home is social communication between peers, family members, and social groups. Interestingly, teens report that social media has helped them feel more confident and outgoing in their relationships, with very few reporting negative effects of using social media. A research study by Common Sense Media found:

> "More than one in four teens say that using their social networking site makes them feel less shy (29%) and more outgoing (28%); one in five says it makes them feel more confident (20%), more popular (19%), and more sympathetic to others (19%); and 15% say it makes them feel better about themselves. By comparison, only 5% say social networking makes them feel less outgoing; 4% feel worse about themselves, less confident, and less popular after using their social networking site; and 3% feel shyer."[57]

The same sample group of teens reported that social media has helped them with relationships, with roughly half (52%) reporting that social media helped with friendships and one-third (37%) reporting that social media helped family relationships. Additionally, a large majority of teens say social media helps them keep in touch with friends they do not regularly see (88%) and get to know classmates better (69%). Only 4% of teens reported that social media had hurt their friendships, and an even smaller percentage (2%) claimed it had hurt family relationships. Teenagers have made it clear that social media is an excellent tool to deepen friendships and family relationships, form new connections with classmates, and build confidence through social connection.

---

57 Common Sense Research, 2012

On a wider level, social media and blogging have provided a platform for cultural exchange, discussion, and social movements among younger generations. Elenna Sonnino, the social media strategist focused on engaging tweens and teens for the social good, commented in an interview, "Teens and this young generation in general want action. They want to be able to see, for better or for worse, really quick action and social media allows them to create positive, meaningful change quickly."[58]

More and more teens are becoming young social activists, using social media as a catalyst for positive change and social and political awareness. In past decades, schools would host coat drives, canned food drives, charity walks. Now, trending hashtags like #unselfie, #crowdfunding, and #disasterandrelief have driven national and global awareness, donations, and change, among teens and the general population.

When children, teens, and young adults use e-mail, video chat, texting, and social media as platforms for communication, tools for moral good, and opportunities for growth and awareness, there is a clear positive impact in the home.

---

58   Wallace, 2014

CHAPTER 4

A Study on Media's Effect on Views of Children

As a part of my post-graduate studies, I conducted a quantitative research study to explore the effects of new media on traditional Catholic values in children. I wanted to specifically observe how media exposure affected children's views regarding marriage and family life, whether those views differed from traditional Catholic values, how parents and children interacted about media, and whether those interactions improved the likelihood of children retaining their Catholic values.

Methods

To achieve the results of my study, I designed an electronic survey for students and their families to take. I sent this survey to the students at three Catholic schools in Birmingham, Alabama, in the United States, and to students at a Catholic school in Kumba, Cameroon. I selected Catholic schools for my survey because I wanted to examine the extent to which media impacts children with a traditional Catholic family background. I contacted the administration of each school for permission to conduct my study before I engaged the students.

The sample population of the survey included middle school and high school students between the ages of 13 and 19. I chose this group for two reasons: first, children this age typically offer a representative sample of children who still live at home; and second, teenagers are one of the age groups that is most engaged in the use of new media.

I have attached the detailed results of my study in the Appendix of this book.

Results within the U.S.

The surveys I conducted in the U.S. portrayed diminishing standards of traditional Catholic family values, which correlated to increases in time spent alone consuming media. According to the trends, children among the ages of 13 and 19 were increasingly engaged in solitary online activities, while time spent with parents and/or siblings was considerably reduced. Given this pattern, families appeared to be living together, but living separate lives. Children who grew up in media-savvy environments spent less time consuming media with peers than expected.

The survey also revealed that certain media content formed children's perception of marriage despite their Catholic background. Nearly 30% of children from typical Catholic homes accepted gay marriage. This statistic is relevant given that over 70% of children in the survey came from closely-knit Catholic families, attended Mass and other church activities at least once a week, and also attended Catholic schools where religious and moral lessons were expected to largely shape their beliefs.

The study found that parents' monitoring of media was an effective means of keeping children safe from the negative influence of the media. A majority of the children who were frequently monitored upheld the traditional view of marriage. On the other hand, belief in traditional marriage steadily reduced among the category of children who were occasionally, rarely, and never monitored. By implication, children who were not monitored were exposed to media content that may have been contrary to traditional Catholic values. The effect of this kind of media consumption may have far reaching consequences on the Catholic wellbeing of children. Unmonitored access to media may allow children access to images of violence, premarital sex, and pornography. Some of these programs also give positive support to divorce, contraceptives, abortion, and same-sex relationships, which are viewed in a negative light by members of the Catholic faith.

Media saturated homes, that is, homes where TV was on around the clock or where children had television sets and access to other gadgets in their bedroom, were less likely to have parental monitoring at all times. Discussing media content at home did have a positive influence on the children's perception of marriage, and parents found that these discussions offered them an alternative way to combat negative media influence that did not interfere too heavily with their busy lives.

Over 80% of the children surveyed felt positive about "friending" or following their ministers on Facebook, Twitter, and other social media networking sites. This data proves that social media is an invaluable tool in evangelization. By having an active presence on social media, priests and pastors would get to know more about the mindsets and concerns of the youth. It also provides a golden opportunity to evangelize and to offer alternative solutions for young people who are lost in their efforts to navigate the new media world. Pastors cannot adequately fulfill this role if they themselves are not up to date about the advances in social media.

Results within Cameroon

Access to media is very different within Cameroon. The survey showed that up to two-thirds of the respondents owned either smart phones or other devices through which they had access to the Internet. One-third of children within the same age group did not have any such device. Daily use of the Internet was also common, though a small percentage of children surveyed had never used the Internet at all. Generally, most of the children spent between one and two hours each time they logged on to the Internet.

Overall, the Cameroonian children were not overly immersed in new technology. The assumption, however, is that Internet services were not readily available, and users may have resorted to cyber cafes, where their usage may have been limited by the cost per hour of service providers. However, the absence of excessive exposure may not have been limited to this assumption. Other factors like family values and discipline may have accounted for this. Without further study, it is impossible to know for sure.

Children mainly used the Internet for research, sending and receiving emails, and reading websites and news. Only a limited percentage of children used the Internet to play video games. This suggests that children mostly used the Internet for studies and educational purposes. Again, the limited availability of Internet exposure could have influenced them to maximize its use for beneficial purposes.

Despite the availability of the Internet, many of the respondents were not familiar with social network sites other than Facebook, and some had no knowledge of social media sites at all.

Traditional family values in Africa were largely intact in terms of time spent together with family members vis-à-vis the media. Children watched TV shows and movies mainly with their parents and siblings. Solitary viewing was minimal. This was likely attributable to the fact that many families owned a single TV set, which was often available in a common room for everyone. On the other hand, it is evident that children who increasingly spent time online were mainly alone and, as a consequence, lessened some family ties.

Overall, children upheld the traditional view of marriage despite their exposure to the media. The deeply rooted traditional perception of marriage was likely a major reason for this belief. However, the effects of media exposure were visibly creeping in among children as up to 21.3% said that marriage was a burden and staying single was better, with another 21% who accepted same-sex unions. This could be interpreted as showing the enormous influence of western media exposure on Cameroonian children. Though same-sex unions are not legalized and are considered a taboo, children may nonetheless identify themselves as homosexual, possibly due to perceptions shaped by a western media diet.

It should be noted that these unconventional views of marriage could also have been caused by a coarse home environment. Children from unstable and broken homes may shun marriage due to failure of their parents to live up to the expectation of traditional teachings on marriage.

Children who were excessively exposed to media deviated from the traditional view of marriage. This trend speaks volumes, and it is likely that a larger sample size including children in public schools would show a more significant outcome. The data showed that where there was frequent parental monitoring, fewer children deviated from traditional views, unlike when monitoring was occasional, rare, or never. I believe it is highly probable that the negative impact on the media in the African family will be strongly felt in the future if parents don't get involved now.

For students who knew about social media, social media proved to be an invaluable tool for evangelization. Young people expressed their willingness to friend or follow their priest or pastor on social media network sites. This was especially true in urban settlements where children lived with the new technology day and night.

Cross-Cultural Analysis: Cameroon and the USA

Generally speaking, there were far more differences than similarities between Cameroonian children and children in the United States.

Similarities

Media exposure and perception of marriage. A vast majority of respondents across the board favored the traditional understanding of marriage as a union between one man and one woman until death do them part. This indicates that the Church,

Catholic education and perhaps traditional family upbringing still play a role in children's perception of marriage despite their exposure to the media.

Media Rules. According to the study, media rules applied to homes in the U.S and in Cameroon. This clearly indicates that parents were (and are) concerned about media exposure and its impact on family values.

Internet Use. Access to and the daily use of the Internet ran across the board on both sides of the world. Many of the children owned smart phones or other devices through which they had access to the Internet on a daily basis. There were differences, though, in regards to how much time was spent online and the kinds of activities in which they engaged.

Parental monitoring. Generally, children in both the U.S. and Cameroon acknowledged that they were monitored by their parents, though in varying degrees.

Media and evangelization. The study showed that children in both countries were very likely to join a church discussion group on social media. They were also willing to 'friend' or follow their priest or pastor on social media.

Church attendance. All respondents attended mass or church service at least once a week. This shows their affinity to the faith.

Differences

Family interactions and the media. The study measured how children interacted with family members amidst the use of media. In the U.S, children were mainly alone when they watched TV shows or movies, while in Cameroon, children were mainly with their parents and siblings when they watched TV or movie shows.

Online activities. The study also showed a vast difference in online activities. In the U.S, children mostly played video games, while in Cameroon, Internet services were used for sending and receiving emails, researching for school, and reading websites for news. This difference was most likely caused by Internet availability differences between the two countries.

Time spent online. Children in the U.S often spent three or more hours each time they logged on to the Internet or when they engaged in some online activity, while many more children in Cameroon spent less than two hours online at a time.

Discussing media content. Parents in the U.S discussed TV shows and movies with their children, whereas in Cameroon, it was rare for parents to discuss media content with their children. Cameroonian children may be less exposed to harmful media content since viewing is a family activity, and they may not have been very media savvy. On the other hand, American kids were more media savvy, and they easily interacted and discussed issues with their parents.

Viewership. Generally, children in the U.S were more exposed to various media outfits than their Cameroonian counterparts. This easy and ready access indicates that viewership time was not only high but also broad. Children in the U.S can be up-to-date with a wide range of current issues, most recent movies, and so on. But this may not be the case with Cameroonian kids.

Same-sex unions and media exposure. According to the survey, U.S kids who spent more time online tended to accept gay unions, whereas exposure time did not affect the perception of marriage of Cameroonian kids.

Parental monitoring. Even though both the respondents in Cameroon and the U.S indicated parental monitoring, children in the U.S were more frequently monitored than their Cameroonian counterparts. The monitoring software and devices that were used in the U.S were not even available in Cameroon. Statistics showed that in Cameroon, children who were rarely or never monitored almost equaled those who were frequently or occasionally monitored.

Marriage is a burden, staying single is better. Up to 21.3% of daily Internet users in Cameroon considered marriage a burden, whereas none of U.S. kids did. This could have been the effect of globalization in terms of the negative impact of some soaps that portray marriage as a burden. Another possible cause could be the effect of the unstable upbringing of children due to divorce.

Discussion: Parents and New Media

The results of my study teach us some important lessons about parents and new media. We can see that media exposure has a significant effect in the lives of families, and this knowledge shows us that we need to carefully consider how to guide the influence of media in our children's lives. Catholic parents in America feel overwhelmed when they try to filter media that does not mesh with their personal and religious values. It truly feels like the onslaught of non-Catholic values through media is a raging flood, whereas Catholic-friendly programming has slowed to a trickle. Even "wholesome family programming," like *Sesame Street*, now shows divorce[59], remarriage, and other non-traditional family structures in an accepting way. How can you maintain a home that participates in new media while still protecting your children's innocence and their Catholic values?

Fortunately, parents can use their influence to help mitigate the influence of media on children's values. Instead of trying to shut out media, Catholic families can and should use media as a teaching tool. By teaching their children to navigate media with a thoughtful and discerning eye, Catholic parents can help their children to grow stronger in their faith and be less vulnerable to messages that contradict their values. This ability is crucial, as Catholic children must be able to navigate and engage with a world that does not always agree with Catholic values while maintaining the truth of their faith. The remainder of this chapter contains some thoughts on the issue of marriage and how parents can counteract the influence of changing media portrayals.

---

59   In 2012, character Abby Cadabby introduced the topic of divorce to the *Sesame Street* audience (Bennett, 2012).

The Problem of American Marriage

There can be no question that U.S society overall seems to be moving further and further away from traditional Catholic values, especially when it comes to traditional marriage. Roughly 1 in every 2 marriages in America will end in divorce. Celebrities make a mockery of the sacrament of marriage by getting married on a whim,[60] or by deciding to get divorced within days of their wedding.[61] Politicians and celebrities flaunt their extramarital affairs in the public eye, and many highly visible couples choose to remain unmarried. Even "defenders of traditional marriage" seem to not understand the definition of traditional marriage: Kim Davis, the Kentucky clerk who refused to grant marriage licenses to same-sex couples, is on her fourth marriage, with three of her marriages having ended in divorce. What a world! And things are not looking like they will improve anytime soon.

Same-sex Marriage

Same-sex attraction, relationships, and marriage are still struggling to gain blanket acceptance in American society, but they gain more ground with every day that passes. The Supreme Court ruling on Obergefell v. Hodges, which legalized same-sex marriage, was a huge blow to supporters of traditional marriage.

In contrast, same-sex sexual activity is still illegal in Cameroon. If caught committing sodomy, homosexuals can face five years of imprisonment and hefty fines. Legislations like this limits the "social acceptability" of open homosexuality within Cameroon, which further limits positive societal views on same-sex marriage. Cameroon has attempted to remain a strong advocate of traditional marriage in other ways as well. According to the U.S State Department, "Divorce cases [in Cameroon] can be brought to customary courts only if the government has not sanctioned the marriage through an official license."[62]

---

60   See: Britney Spears
61   See: Kim Kardashian
62   U.S. Department of State, 2008

However, even traditionally Catholic countries are striking traditional marriage laws from their books due to social pressure. In the Republic of Ireland, divorce became legal in 1996.[63] Ireland actually legalized same-sex marriage in May 2015, a full month before the U.S. did. And Ireland is not alone in its decision to legalize non-traditional marriages. Traditionally Catholic countries have been legalizing same-sex marriage since 2005, when Spain became the first traditionally Catholic nation to do so.[64]

With even traditionally Catholic countries abandoning their moral principles, how can we expect more from America? We can pray that Americans will regain their moral footing and do what is righteous, but until Americans are able to know God's love and His truth, rulings like Obergefell v. Hodges and Roe v. Wade will stand. As Catholics, we must fight politically for what we know in our hearts to be right, and as parents, we must guide and teach our children so that they may join the communion of Saints.

Resources

Parents can find many examples of media guidelines online; some of these are listed in Appendix E. I encourage you to edit these to reflect the specific needs of your family. As suggested above, you may find a media agreement or pledge helpful. I have included a sample media agreement in the Appendix of this book. Feel free to tailor it to fit your family, or make your own!

However you choose to approach your media plan, remember that as parents, you are the first and most important educators, especially in regards to media. Your involvement in your child's digital life is essential to their success and moral growth.

Remember, you are never alone in trying to help your children to grow into devout Catholics. Your community, your Church, your friends, and your family will all be useful resources as you

---

63   Wikipedia, 2016
64   Liu, 2015

and your children work to balance media consumption with the traditional values of your faith. See Chapter 8 of this book for more suggestions on living with new media as a contemporary Christian family.

CHAPTER 5

The African Family
Challenges, Hopes, and Expectations

In addition to the challenges they face as a Catholic family, the Cameroonian family faces additional challenges, as Cameroonian culture and U.S. culture divest further and further. Already, diaspora members believe that family and loved ones in Cameroon "don't understand" their struggles—which alienates members of the diaspora and makes second- and third-generation diaspora members less likely to communicate with, identify with, and agree with family who are still in Cameroon. The pressure to become more American forces Cameroonian immigrants to stretch their cultural and religious values.

Bush-Falling

The studies I conducted are yet another example of how traditional African family values have been impacted by cultural globalization through the media. Many Africans in the diaspora are becoming more and more comfortable with all aspects of the western way of life. In the distant past, Cameroonian students and civil servants only longed to undertake further studies abroad and return home. However, these days, many Cameroonians find themselves having "Bush-falling" syndrome. Bush-falling is the craving to travel abroad in search for greener pastures. Bush-falling syndrome associates having a better life and better job with western civilization.

Africans have often regarded "Bush fallers" with high esteem, but some of that respect has dwindled recently due to the exposure of fake promises and involvement with shady deals that some Bush fallers have made. These include, among others, deceiving young girls about marriage and projecting a false image of themselves, especially when it comes to their wealth. Despite this tarnished image of Bush fallers, thousands upon thousands of Africans still seek visas so that they, too, can "fall bush." At least one out of every two families in Cameroon and other parts of Africa have children or a close family member living abroad.

Our Culture is Threatened at Home and Abroad

This cultural mix presents a real threat and challenge to traditional African values on love, marriage, and family. Despite the benefits that the global village phenomenon can bring, there is also the downside that empties Africans of their very identity, their inestimable cultural heritage, and much more. Africans want to live in the Western style, forgetting that they have their own cultural identity and that Western realities are not the same as those of Africa. For example, many Africans abroad have embraced the redefinition of marriage and family that the media has relayed to them. Marriage is reduced to a trivial contract that can be broken whenever it suits us.

The negative impact of globalization is not simply Africa's problem; it equally poses a challenge to the Church in our times. The Church is called to be the torch bearer on matters of life, love, marriage, and family. Yet, these foundational beliefs of the Christian faith are now more badly scrutinized than they ever have been.

According to the Christian faith, family is not merely a human institution. The second creation account highlights the communal character of mankind: "it is not good that man should be alone; I will make him a helper fit for him."[65] This helper draws man out of his solitude and introduces him to the logic of

---

65   Gen. 2:18

mutual solidarity as a sign of God's goodness toward him. This reciprocity forms the bond and the basis of social solidarity and the human guarantee of the future of societies.

Society begins in the family. Within the family, all men, all women, and all communities discover the transcendental dimension of their being. The family reminds them that something precedes us, or rather someone is at the origin of our existence, which consequently appears as a plan and acquires a vocational dimension.

In the spirit of the best African traditions, the family's existence always starts from a man and a woman, who by founding a home, give birth to ties of affinity, mutual assistance, and peace between families and between different ethnic and tribal communities. Above and beyond the diversity of its forms, in Africa and throughout the world, the family shows its social reason for being: to be the crucible of life and of a society of harmony and peace.

When the meaning of marriage and family is distorted, the unfortunate consequences include the lack of respect for human life and the dignity of the human person. It is within this context that it is often said the family has become the object of attack in contemporary society. Archbishop Denis Amuzu-Dzakpah of Lome says that we must arm ourselves appropriately to engage in and continue to the finish the noble battle to save the family at all costs. The Archbishop goes on to say that, within the Holy Family that was just beginning, the Child Jesus was threatened with death by Herod from the very first days of his coming into the world in Bethlehem. Our Africa was a land of refuge, welcome, and hospitality for the family of Jesus, Mary, and Joseph.[66]

Paradoxically, while Africans are losing hold of their fundamental family values, the Church is giving attention to Africa as the hope of the world in the matters of marriage and family. According to Saint John Paul II, Africa is the continent that must

---

66 Christ's New Homeland-Africa: contributions to the synod on the family by African pastors, 2015

teach us by fresh efforts to rediscover and to respect meaning and inestimable value of all human life. He explained:

> "In African culture and tradition, the role of family is everywhere held to be fundamental. Open to this sense of the family, of love and respect for life, the African loves children, who are joyfully welcomed as gifts of God. 'The sons and daughters of Africa love life…The peoples of Africa respect the life which is conceived and born. They rejoice in this life. They reject the idea that it can be destroyed, even when the so-called "progressive civilizations" would like to lead them in this direction…' Africans show their respect for human life until its natural end and keep elderly parents and relatives within the family."[67]

Challenges to Family Stability in Africa

Family stability in Africa is no longer what is it used to be. In addition to the practice of polygamy and forced marriages, divorce is also on the rise, caused by a combination of factors including adultery; spousal abuse; the rejection of fertility; sterility; the interference of in-laws in the couple's affairs; and ethnic, religious, and cultural differences.

It is worth looking at some of these problems that are affecting the African family:

Forced Marriages

Forced marriages are nothing new, whether in Africa or in the rest of the world. Before the 18th century, families would arrange marriages, often with one or both parties being unwilling participants in the match.[68] Forced marriages, and arranged marriages in general, fell out of favor in the Western world with the rise of romanticism, i.e., "marrying for love," but these

---

67   John Paul II, 1995
68   O'Brien, 2008

aromantic marital practices are still alive and thriving in many parts of the world. Legislators have made strong efforts towards outlawing forced marriage, especially in sub-Saharan Africa, but the line between what is "forced" and what is merely "arranged" is often blurry.

In 2005, The *New York Times* published an article recounting the ordeal of young girls whose families forced them into marriages.[69] In villages throughout northern Malawi, girls are often married at or before puberty to whomever their fathers choose, sometimes to husbands as much as half a century older. Many of those same girls later choose lifelong misery over divorce because custom decrees that children in patriarchal tribes belong to the father.

In interviews, fathers and daughters unapologetically explained the rationales for forced, intergenerational unions:

"Uness Nyambi, of the village of Wiliro, said she was betrothed as a child so her parents could finance her brother's choice of a bride. Now about 17, she has two children, the oldest nearly 5, and a husband who guesses he is 70. 'Just because of these two children, I cannot leave him,' she said.

"Beatrice Kitamula, 19, was forced to marry her wealthy neighbor, now 63, five years ago because her father owed another man a cow. 'I was the sacrifice,' Ms. Kitamula said, holding back tears. She likened her husband's comfortable compound of red brick houses in Ngana village to a penitentiary. 'When you are in prison,' she said, 'you have no rights.'"[70]

Malawi is by no means the only country in sub-Saharan Africa to engage in the practice of forced marriage. Cameroon is one of the many nations that also participates in this commoditization of women and girls. While forced marriages are

---

69   Lafraniere, 2005
70   Lafraniere, 2005

illegal in Cameroon, as they are in most of the world, many Cameroonians surveyed by the International Women's Health Coalition knew "more about the traditional and religious norms that legitimize the practice [of forced marriage] than about the laws against it."[71] Of those same survey respondents, a distressing 89% believed that girls should have their first menstruation under their husband's roof instead of under their parents'. Given that the latest a girl may start menstruating is 16 years old, only one year older than Cameroon's legal age for marriage with parental consent, these views clearly encourage and endorse child marriage, which can never be fully consensual.

Enforcement of existing laws, increasing education for girls about their legal rights, and changing traditional cultural and religious norms are the only ways for girls to escape the systemic horror of forced marriage. This is a problem for all mankind, and it is a detriment to the sacrament of marriage and to the bonds of family.

Adultery

Adultery is having sexual relations with a person other than one's spouse. Adultery is one of the most frequent causes of separation and divorce. In some cultures, particularly that of the Bamele'ke's, adultery, especially of the wife, is considered a scandal and is fraught with consequences for the wife who has committed adultery. However, among the Bamile'ke's as in other cultures in African societies, the husband's infidelity is tolerated because a Bamile'ke' man is "by nature" polygamous. It is not a question here of legitimizing polygamy; that is a practice contrary to the law of marriage that advocates monogamy.[72] The Scripture tells us, "Therefore a man shall leave his father and mother and cleave to his wife and the two shall become on flesh."[73] This passage doesn't suggest that only wives are subject

71   International Women's Health Coalition, 2016
72   Christ's New Homeland-Africa: contributions to the synod on the family by African pastors, 2015
73   Gen. 2:24

to the law of fidelity! On the contrary, it is clear that spouses are bound to be faithful to each other.

Sterility and the Rejection of Fertility

In African culture, the primary purpose of marriage is procreation. In couples where procreation is hampered, whether voluntarily or involuntarily, the chances of their marriages lasting until death are greatly reduced. For the Catholic Church, the birth of a child to a couple is not what makes marriage valid: children are a gift from God, not a right of the couple. However, it must be noted that the rejection of fertility through the use of contraceptives is still a serious violation of the law of marriage, which wishes the spouses to be ready to accept all the children they can raise decently.

Interference by In-Laws, Especially in Regards to Ethnic, Religious, and Cultural Differences

The interference of in-laws in marriages is a real problem in Africa, especially considering that marriage usually involves the coming together of two families. When the mother-in-law lives with the married couple, there is a significant chance that the marriage will end in failure. How many useless quarrels end up killing love? The in-laws, very often, are the ones who show the difference of social class or ethnic group, to the point of creating frustrations for the couple that lead to separation only a few years after the wedding. Sadly, parents can fan the flames of divorce where they had not wished their son or daughter to marry someone who is not of their clan. The ill of tribalism is still having its toll on marriages in Africa.

The African Christian Family

Amidst these challenges, the African is also called to conversion; only an African family that has been evangelized can live up to the calling of marriage and family life. This would require giving up fatal traditional practices that do not foster the dignity of women and girls as created in the image and likeness of God. Africans must rise beyond any form of enslaving girls, tribalism, and other ills that are contrary to the vocation of the Christian family. Saint Paul's exhortation to the Christians of Philippi is relevant: "Finally brethren, whatever is true, whatever is honorable, whatever is just, whatever is pure, whatever is lovely, whatever is gracious, if there is any excellence, if there is anything worthy of praise, think about these things."[74] Saint Peter on his part, calls upon Christ's faithful to conduct themselves honorably in the world, so as to silence critics and to lead all to praise God.[75]

There is also a need to transfigure the traditional values of the African family, which the Teams of Our Lady (E'quipes Notre-Dame) of Senegal point out in a document dealing with "African Values and Christianity" and "Values adopted by the Senegalese." They note that the African Christian Family is the institution capable of integrating the positive values of traditional Africa. We can make a new world in a new Africa by rediscovering all the values and strengths of the continent.[76]

---

74   Phil. 4:8
75   1 Pet. 2:11-12
76   Christ's New Homeland-Africa: contributions to the synod on the family by African pastors, 2015

CHAPTER 6

African Families in America

Cameroonians at home tend to have many of the same questions about their friends and family abroad: "Why do they speak and behave like westerners when they visit home?" "Why are they not committed to religious observances, such as church attendance and other spiritual activities, in the same way they are when they're home?" "Why is the path to divorce so easily trodden abroad?" "Why are extended family members not closely knit out there?" "Why do they have few kids?"

The answers to these questions vary from case to case. And though it is not the scope of this work to capture the nitty gritty of such concerns, they all impact the stability of family life in one way or the other. Suffice it to say that the social, cultural, and economic changes of moving to the United States can be drastic and enormous, yet everyone must survive. The economic dynamics in a capitalist system can lead to excessive financial pressures on some immigrants, who must take on two or more jobs and work for long hours in order to pay debts, bills, taxes, and so on. There are several economic and social factors that contribute to the new way of life that Africans in the diaspora adopt. Many Africans find themselves either in middle income class or the lower income class, yet burdened by onerous responsibilities. Despite their efforts, some are still not able to afford health insurance, which the American government now requires each resident to carry—or face a fine.

Given this reality, life's meaning revolves around making money to make ends meet. When people have a disagreement, it usually ends up like this: "You can go to hell; after all, do you pay my bills?" Like the Scripture says, where your heart is, there your treasure will be also. In this way, many African cultural values have been relegated while immigrants have wholeheartedly embraced the new culture with its good, bad, and ugly sides. This partly explains why extended family disintegration, divorce, and lack of religious commitments are common.

Interviews with Some African Families in the Diaspora

As a part of my investigations into the effects of media on children's views of traditional marriage, I conducted several interviews with families from the Cameroonian diaspora. While these interviews do not cover the wide variety of experiences faced by Cameroonian immigrants, they may illustrate some of the struggles that are common among our community.

Interview with Vivian Bongla of Gaithersburg, MD.

I conducted this interview in June of 2014, with Ms. Vivian Bongla at her Gaithersburg residence in Maryland. Vivian was originally from the Littoral region of Cameroon. She came to the United States in 2009 in search for greener pastures. She was a single parent living with her daughter, Chantal, who joined her in 2013. She did part-time jobs, and she was also enrolled in college. She is a Catholic Christian.

Interviewer: How do you monitor your child's use of the media, like the kind of TV programs and shows she watches?

Vivian: I don't have time. I mean it is difficult to do, as we have it back in Cameroon. I have my job, I have to go to work. I also go to school…school does not end in this country, you know (she laughs). When I come back I am tired, and I have to start preparing for the next day. Once in a while we meet in the living room, but it is usually very brief. We watch television, and I fall asleep on the couch. I have two jobs, so I have to work a lot because I must pay my car notes, bills, and I have a project in Cameroon. After ten more years I should go back home to live a real family life. Here, no!"

Interviewer: Do you discuss media use with your daughter?

Vivian: I would have loved to, but like I said, I don't have the time for that. She, too, is busy with her school and work. I just believe she is doing the right thing because I don't have the energy to follow her up with the many things I have to do.

Interviewer: Do you have media rules at home?

Vivian: I have been thinking about that, because I remember how we used to watch television together with our parents in our house in Douala. And that really helped us to watch only educative programs and the news. Now I have to do something to help my daughter.

Interviewer: Apart from Sunday mass, are you able to take part in other spiritual activities?

Vivian: I try to go to Church every Sunday and sometimes during the week. I have gone through very hard times here, and I have come to know God more through my experience. In this country? Without God, I would be finished. I belong to an online prayer group we call prayer line. It is Catholic, and we talk about the saints also. So I do my best.

Interview with Chantal

After interviewing Vivian, I interviewed her daughter, Chantal. Chantal was 17 years old. She had lived in the U.S. for one year with her mom, and she was a student. She also held a part-time job. She owned an iPhone and a personal computer through which she had access to the Internet.

Interviewer: How often do watch TV programs or TV shows with your mom?

Chantal: I am new here, everything is just fast. I see my mother early in the morning and sometimes late at night. We communicate often by text message. Sometimes I tell her good night by text message because I go to sleep before she comes

53

back from work. I am happy that our phones here have Internet because it keeps me connected with friends back home. But we watch TV together once in a while during weekends. I usually chat a lot on Facebook. Sometimes it gets boring. But I have no choice. That's how I try to keep myself busy.

Interviewer: What do you mostly use the Internet for?

Chantal: I often chat with my friends on Facebook. I feel very lonely sometimes. I also watch movies and play some video games. Sometimes I use it also for research.

Interviewer: How much time do you spend online each time you log on?

Chantal: Well, I can't really tell you, but I spend much time because that's the only way I occupy myself when I don't have school and no work. Sometimes in one day, I can use the Internet six to seven times. Anytime I am free that is the place I go to, the Internet.

Interview with Mrs. Eunice Ambe

I conducted this interview on November 26, 2015, at the Ambe family residence in Baltimore, Maryland. Mr. Oliver Ambe and Mrs. Eunice Oliver had three children, Aloysius (14), Loretta (12), and Roberline (9). Aloysius and Loretta owned iPhones through which they accessed the Internet. Mrs. Ambe Eunice was a nurse. She was a member of the Catholic Women's Association and a devout Catholic. She came into the U.S. in 2007, and the rest of her family joined her in 2014. When I mentioned that I was coming to speak to her children about media and the family, she immediately started speaking passionately about the family media practices.

Mrs. Ambe: We don't allow them to watch from Monday to Friday because they have to do their homework. With the Internet services at home, they have to do only their homework, and we ensure that they don't go to inappropriate sites. I am aware of all the bad stuff going on, so I always tell them to be careful. We have told them not to accept friend requests on Facebook from people they don't know. We censor the programs that they watch, and we try to watch the news together during weekends. We also watch the Eternal Word Television (EWTN) to edify our faith. We always encourage them to watch television together. But you see, I cannot speak for them because Aloysius and Loretta have their own phones.

Interviewer: Do you discuss the media with your children?

Mrs. Ambe: Yes, I talk with them all the time to watch out the kind of things they do on the Internet. I try to remind them every time about the values of our culture, like, respect and obedience, and spending time with siblings. I think they are doing fine.

Interviewer: What about Church?

Mrs. Ambe: (She laughs.) You know I belong to Mama Maria. We don't joke with Church here, Father. The only problem is that we cannot always go together because of our work schedules, but we don't miss mass Sundays. Sometimes I go with the children and their father also goes with them when I can't attend the same mass with them. But we don't miss mass.

About time together, Mrs. Ambe says it was hard for them to meet up for meals within the week as the custom is back home. But they ate together during the weekend.

Speaking about family Prayer, Mrs. Ambe said they made a lot of effort to maintain their family devotion. They had "Covenant time," which was the time in the evening that they came together to pray. Generally, they tried to keep the disciplinary customs of home. For example, when Mrs. Ambe would speak to them, they would stay quiet and listen.

I asked Aloysius what he mostly does online.

Aloysius: I mostly chat with my friends and family on Facebook. I post my pictures for my friends in Cameroon. I miss many of my friends in Cameroon. Here I don't have friends, and I see that life here is different. People are just on their own.

Interviewer: How often do you go online?

Aloysius: I can't really tell, but I do it at least four times a day.

Interviewer: How much time do you spend each time you log on to the net?

Aloysius: Sometimes I spend thirty minutes and sometimes 1 hour. It depends, if I meet my friends online, I spend more time.

Loretta's use of the media is similar to her older brother's, but with a few differences:

Loretta: I mostly go online to check my grades, to do my homework, then when I have free time, I look at the pictures my friends post on social media… Life is lonely here, I can't go out and meet friends in the neighborhood as I did back in Cameroon. I also miss my church group a lot. I am a member of the cadets of Mary Immaculate.

Interview with Martin Fienkeng and Mathilda Fienkeng

Another interview I conducted was with Martin Fienkeng, Mathilda Fienkeng, and their family. They lived in Woodstock, Maryland. Martin was Executive Director of Information Technology at Laureate Education, and Mathilda was a Supervisory Regulatory Officer (Pharmacist) at the U.S. Food and Drug Administration (FDA). They had three children, aged 15, 13, and 11 years old at the time of the interview. Martin had been in the U.S. for 12 years, and Mathilda had been there for 9 years.

Interviewer: How do you monitor your children's use of the media and the kind of TV programs or TV shows they watch?

Mathilda: Based on the type of media, and it has evolved as they grow older and gain more accountability.

For TV, generally, no TV during Monday through Thursday. When they were younger, we watched TV with them to determine what we wanted them to watch or not. Once that was established, we then went broader and determined what channels they can watch, and then finally they were required to ask permission to watch any new shows outside of the allowed channels. Now that they are older, they know they can watch shows that are teenage shows, or PG13 shows or movies.

No TVs in their bedrooms, and the family TV and family computers are in communal family spaces.

For computers, rules, rules, rules of expectations, accountability, responsibility, and potential loss of privileges or consequences. When they were younger, we set limits in rules, but also we set up the network to log their computers off the network every 2 hours. But as they got older, they need computers for school work.

To monitor media use, I occasionally check their cell phone data usage times, and it time stamps when they access it and how long they were on it. I have done this maybe 2 times in the last year when I had concerns that someone was not having enough sleep. They usually use the computers in the main family area.

Above all, trust is our biggest rule in the house.

Interviewer: Do you discuss media use with them? If yes, kindly share with me what you talk about with them.

Mathilda: Yes we do, and it has evolved over time based on their needs and ages. For our daughters, they love reading, writing, and belong to online writing blogs where you post your writings and get readers to comment. We talk about the dangers of the Internet, people posing as teenagers, and discuss ways to never disclose personal information. The high-schooler is the only one who can post stories for herself or her sister. They let us see it first and approve it.

Interviewer: Do you have media rules? Examples, if you do. This would include some restrictions, limitations, days and periods of exposure.

Mathilda: Yes we have media rules. Emails and Facebook: Before email accounts are established, we discuss general rules regarding not opening emails or responding if you do not know them. As parents, we have your email passwords and can ask you to see your email account at any time. For Facebook, we had my high-schooler read up on the Internet about the dangers of Facebook and social media, and come up with rules that will be necessary to be safe on the Internet. She came up with a better document than we would have thought of. For example, if you wonder if something you are about to post will be a problem, then it likely is a problem. If you choose to post pictures of yourself, first show us to ensure it is appropriate and after you have done so for a long time and feel confident you can make right choices, then you can do so without our feedback. Note that she does not post pictures of herself anyway. Never accept friend requests from strangers or even family members without discussing with us—because not all "aunties" or "uncles" should know what is going on in your life (we did not even think of this but agreed with it). Be sensible and kind to others even if they have different views. She can post all her Catholic faith beliefs and be proud of them, and let others know what you stand for... but will not insult or condemn others if they post items that are different with her views. Be true to who you are and reserve judgment.

Mathilda: During the week, use of media should be only after homework and chores are completed, and before bedtime. During the weekend, they can use it when they are done with their chores. We also require outdoor time each day—20 basketball baskets or ride your bike in the neighborhood. My son is very good on this, but the girls...not so much. The high schooler has a lot of work and belongs to color guard at school—so she does a lot of exercise and has less free time at all even during the weekend. Her school work load is very challenging—she has all advance GT and Honors classes.

Interviewer: What are some of the challenges you face in regulating your children's exposure to the media? Use of phones, personal computers, TV shows.

Mathilda: Mobile devices go with them to their rooms. They are growing old, and we have to give them the opportunity to learn to be accountable and responsible but still be able to monitor. It is a challenge to balance between trust and verifying. They know we trust them a lot, and they also know that we expect a lot of accountability from them.

Mathilda: For TV, no concerns. In fact, I think they could benefit from a little more news TV. But they do not like watching the news or TV in general. I think they miss out on what is happening in the world. When they do watch TV, it is generally educational and science shows that are related to geography, engineering, math, etc.

Personal computers, etc., it is hard to limit the time for them because most of the time, they are using it to do useful things that are educational. My oldest loves to write stories and reads a lot online. My youngest loves to use the computer for computer graphics, computer coding. All three of them love to use YouTube to watch their favorite YouTube channels related to mathematics and science. So it is challenging to decide how much new knowledge is too good. More so, they usually do this together, which helps with their bonding as siblings.

Interviewer: Apart from Sunday Mass attendance, do you belong to any Church group?

Mathilda belongs to the co-catechist for religious education at our parish for 3rd graders. Anne-Marie belongs to Life Teen group at our parish. She is also a Teen Aide for 3rd grade for religious education. Ralph and Anne-Marie are altar servers at Church.

Part 2 of the interview involved the children, who responded independently.

Interviewer: How often do you use the Internet? You can write about the number of times a day or per week.

Anne- Marie: I use the Internet daily. Probably between 14–20 individual times a week.

Ralph: 2 or 3 times a day.

Dasi: A lot. Every day.

Interviewer: What do you usually use the Internet for? Video games, chats on Facebook, movies, research, etc. Kindly write about your activities online.

Anne- Marie: I usually watch videos or listen to music and write and read stories. I also research words, topics for school, and random fields of study (out of interest). I spend the most time on YouTube, Songza, and Google Docs.

Ralph: Mostly for entertainment. Usually playing solitaire or watching videos on YouTube.

Dasi: YouTube, coding computer programs, games, reading, making papers and presentations for school. Mostly for schoolwork.

Interviewer: Whenever you log on to the Internet, how much time do spend online?

Anne-Marie: Whenever I go on, I usually spend an hour or 2 on the Internet in some way.

Ralph: I usually spend about 3 hours or less.

Dasi: I always do about 2–3 hours in the Internet in some way.

Interviewer: Do you watch TV shows or movies mainly alone or with your parents and siblings? You can write about the times you watch alone and the times you watch with your parents and siblings.

Anne-Marie: I mainly watch TV with my parents or siblings. I rarely do watch TV overall. I'll usually watch a cartoon with my siblings and a movie, documentary, or science program with my dad.

Ralph: Alone. I watch TV a lot of the time.

Dasi: I rarely watch TV. When I do, I watch science shows usually with my family. I watch cartoons alone.

Interviewer: Do you think that the media rules in your home are stricter than those of your friends? If yes, explain.

Anne-Marie: Yes. I am not allowed to watch TV or use the Internet leisurely during the week. Most people I know have hour limits, if that. When it comes to what we watch, we have our own common sense as to what we should watch. (I don't think have a problem with any of it at all.)

Ralph: No. They're pretty even with everyone else's.

Dasi: Yes. I'm 11, and I don't have a phone or any social media accounts. Not that it's a bad thing.

Analysis

These interviews clearly bring out the different challenges immigrant families face in the diaspora. Family values thrive depending on the nature of work and economic status. It is certain that where family members lack a decent or regular job, time with family could become as scarce as water in the Sahara. Additionally, when parents have to combine school and work, life becomes a matter of hit and rush. All these circumstances affect family life and commitment to religious activities.

As for the migrants who have lived in the U.S. for a long time, and who through toil, have acquired a well-paid job, the situation is completely different. Parents of these families do not exceed the minimum work hours per week. These are considered the more stable families in terms of economic status. This increased availability equates to more family time, regulation of the media, and family values are generally upheld.

Loneliness

From the interviews I've conducted and from my personal experience, I know that one of the most difficult things for Cameroonian families in America is the sense of loneliness that comes with uprooting yourself from your friends and family to move to a new land. Children in particular feel this loneliness. As you read, the children I spoke with told me, "Life is lonely here. I can't go out and meet friends in the neighborhood as I did back in Cameroon," and "I miss many of my friends in Cameroon. Here, I don't have friends, and I see that life here is different. People are just on their own."

Children from these homes have no option other than to develop coping mechanisms, and one of them is living in the virtual world. Consider, for instance, those who migrated as teenagers: it is a challenging transition from the booming social life in Cameroon, interaction with friends and neighbors, to a new of life of solitary. Consequently, they resort to online activities such as video gaming, chatting, and so on. Moreover, they also try to stay connected with friends back home.

Adults feel lonely and isolated as well in this new world. They don't fit in with American culture, but they also no longer fit in with African culture. Friends and family at home act shocked by how living abroad changes their loved ones, without trying to understand why their loved ones have begun acting more like westerners. They seldom realize the pressures their loved ones face just to make ends meet in America, and there is just not enough time in the day for emigrant relatives to explain how and why life in America has changed them. Often, the easiest thing to do is to just not call home and embrace the loneliness.

Fortunately, modern media can help! This is one of the many great goods that God has woven into new media: the chance to connect with friends and family in all corners of the earth. Children and adults alike can use tools like Facebook and messaging apps to stay in contact with their Cameroonian loved ones. These tools let you share the triumphs and struggles in your life with the people who care, and they help to keep you connected to your Cameroonian roots. It's a far cry from being able to go next door and talk, but thoughtful use of media can help keep you and your family from feeling quite so isolated and lonely in your new home.

Retaining Traditional Values

In Cameroon, there is nothing more important than one's family and community. We lived in tightly-knit circles of relatives and neighbors whom we loved as though they were blood. We respect our elders, and we care for them as a community when they can no longer care for themselves. We also love and honor God and His Church, and seek to follow Her teachings all of our days.

These values are very different from the values held near and dear by many Americans, and it is a struggle to instill these values in our children when we are separated from our supporting family and community. American media, as you have seen, does not help us in this endeavor; it follows its agenda of depicting its own version of morality and family values, which often clash with ours.

Expectations

Life in Cameroon and the United States will always be different. The two countries are on vastly different continents and have vastly different histories, which guide and influence them from day to day. Their politics, economy, and social makeup are also different. But if there is anything we have learned from the advent of new media, it is this: for all of our differences, we are all human, and we are more alike than we realize.

New media is helping to keep Cameroonian families together over the vast physical and cultural distance that moving to America brings. These days, it is easy for grandchildren to Skype or FaceTime with their grandparents, aunts, uncles, and cousins back home in Cameroon. Family and friends can keep in touch and up-to-date on each other's lives and struggles through social media platforms.

This ability to communicate is benefitting the Cameroonian family in three ways: first, it is helping family back home to understand some of the struggles their family in America are facing each day; second, it helps Cameroonian children abroad stay in touch with their traditions and the values that Cameroonian families hold dear; and third, it helps to relieve some of the alienation and loneliness that comes with uprooting one's family and moving across the world. As 3G Internet becomes more widely available in Cameroon, communication like this is bound to increase, to everyone's benefit.

It is my prayer that Cameroonian families will be able to embrace these benefits of new media and incorporate them into their lives while successfully mitigating the risks of new media. The following guidelines are a great starting point for creating a healthy relationship with new media, especially for your children.

CHAPTER 7

How Families Can Live with New Media

The United States is an ever-evolving social landscape, and families find it difficult to manage the influence of the media, which mirrors and encourages those changes. In previous chapters, we have discussed that parents can help to mitigate new media's influence on impressionable children by offering guidelines, rules, and the knowledge of how to understand and decipher media messages. See Appendix E for a list of online resources for parents. This chapter will give you a more in-depth guide on how you can create a family environment in which the Scripture and new media can peacefully coexist.

Start with God

As parents, you are the primary and most important educators of your children. They will learn much of what they know about the "moderate, critical, watchful, and prudent use of the media"[77] from you. But how should you start teaching them? As the Scripture says, "In the beginning was the Word: the Word was with God and the Word was God."[78] As with all things in this life, we must first look to God and His Sacred Scripture for guidance before we start trying to teach our children about media.

Pope Francis emphasized in his October 2013 address that parents (and all teachers) must find nourishment in the Word before educating their children. He states:

---

77 Francis, 2013
78 John 1:1

"Fathers and mothers need to be talking about the Word of God! And I think of catechists and of all those who are involved in education: if their hearts have not been warmed by the Word, how can they warm the hearts of others, of children, of youth, of adults? It is not enough just to read the Sacred Scriptures, we need to listen to Jesus who speaks in them: it is Jesus himself who speaks in the Scriptures. We need to be receiving antennas that are tuned into the Word of God, in order to become broadcasting antennas! One receives and transmits. It is the Spirit of God who makes the Scriptures come alive, who makes us understand them deeply and in accord with their authentic and full meaning!"[79]

The words of Christ offer parents strength in raising their children and guidance in educating them. The Second Vatican Council taught that "if the media are to be correctly employed, it is essential that all who use them know the principles of the moral order and apply them faithfully."[80] There is no better place to learn the principles of moral order than in Scripture, at Mass, and in the Sacraments.

Church Resources

After consulting Scripture, there still remains an important question, how do parents apply the precepts of the faith to media?

Different popes, councils, and commissions have published a variety of Church resources and guidelines in a number of documents over the years. These include, among others, Communio et Progressio, Inter Mirifica, Aetatis Novae, and some of the Popes' letters on World Days of Communication. While some of these documents may be dense, they are well worth your time and effort.

Your priest will also be an excellent resource in your efforts to help your children to view media through a faith-based lens.

79   Francis, 2013
80   Inter Mirifica, 1963

Talk to him about your efforts, and seek his advice on additional information and resources you can use.

Be There for Your Kids

The Scripture and the Church are crucial parts of parents' media education strategies. However, without parents there to introduce them to their children, the Scripture and the Church cannot do much to offer children an enriching and morally acceptable household media environment. Parents have to be there for their kids if they want to educate them and guide their media consumption.

I understand—this life is full of worldly cares. Many parents struggle to find time for a variety of reasons. But regardless of your struggles, you must prioritize making time for your children. After all, it is only through your guidance that your children will grow into the kind, loving, and devout Catholics you wish them to be.

The easiest way to ensure that you and your family will be able to spend time together is to schedule that time together. Many families find that having nightly dinners as a family is a great way to put aside quality time even in the face of hectic lives. I encourage you to look at your family schedule to determine what will work best for you and your family.

Be Interested in Your Children's Interests

According to the Pontifical Commission for the Means of Social Communication, "It is never too early to start encouraging in children artistic taste, a keen critical faculty and a sense of personal responsibility that is based on sound morality. They need all these so that they can use discrimination in choosing from the publications, films and broadcasts that are set before them."[81] As they grow, however, your children will begin to naturally show a preference for specific media based on their personal interests.

---

81   Communio et Progressio, 1971

You can, of course, guide and mold these interests, but I also encourage you to take the time to listen to your child when they talk about what interests them. Ask questions about the programming they like and why they like it. This information will provide you with a base you can use to help your children learn about moral responsibility in their media habits while using examples they enjoy talking about.

Discuss Media Intelligently with Children

During your family time, be certain to discuss media with your children. Start with their interests, and bridge into morality issues and the benefits of being selective in what media one chooses to consume.

You will have to tailor your discussion based on the age of your children, but remember that even the youngest children can benefit from talking about media intelligently. Ask questions about the content and its messages, then ask questions about how those messages relate to your Catholic faith. If you allow older children to interact with media that offer complicated views that conflict with Catholic values, discuss how those views made them feel about their values, and reinforce God's truth as a part of the discussion.

Your efforts should be geared toward creating an interactive media atmosphere, where family members and friends can discuss the meaning and ideas derived from the media. In this way, television and media become resources for conversations in family social interactions and a means by which your family can structure their time together.[82]

I encourage you to be fully engaged in these conversations. Practice active listening to understand both the words your children are saying and the things they aren't saying. You can guide the conversation, but let your kids do most of the talking so that they feel engaged in the process.

---

82   Lull, 1980

Create Regulations as a Family

Parents also need to regulate the use of media in a clear and direct way for the benefit of children. This would include planning and scheduling media use, strictly limiting the time children devote to media, making entertainment a family experience, putting some media entirely off limits, and periodically excluding all of them for the sake of other family activities. Above all, parents should be a good example to children by their own thoughtful and selective use of media. Often they will find it helpful to join with other families to study and discuss the problems and opportunities presented by the use of the media. Families should be outspoken in telling producers, advertisers, and public authorities what they like and dislike.

Most families find it's helpful to write a family media plan, involving the children in creating specific and concrete media guidelines for the home. It is important to cover all forms of media, focusing on the following:

Begin with setting screen time limits according to age. The American Academy of Pediatrics recommends that children between the ages of 3 and 18 use screens for a maximum of two hours daily; and kids younger than three should avoid screens altogether, including television screens.[83]

- Cover what programs are acceptable to watch and what types of programming to avoid. It is important to discuss why children should avoid shows with violence and sexual content, while clearly explaining the consequences of a poor choice.

- Designate "media-free" times and places. Many families find that they interact more when they ban media at meal times and bedtimes, as well as during family social events and gatherings. If you and your family are having trouble unplugging, make a game

83 American Academy of Pediatrics, 2015

of it: put all of your cell phones or media devices in the middle of the table at meal times. Whoever asks to look at their phone first has to wash dishes after dinner!

- Determine what is and isn't the proper use of the Internet. Take time to discuss the dangers of chat rooms, pornography, cyber-bullying, etc.

- Employ an Internet filter to monitor online activity and block undesirable content.

- Set strict guidelines regarding social media use, focusing on the positive aspects of socializing within the set boundaries. It is important to set rules regarding posting personal information, friending strangers, and posting appropriate pictures. It is equally important for parents to understand the basics of popular social media sites like Twitter, Facebook, and Instagram.

Make Space for God

Find ways to incorporate Bible lessons, scripture, or worship music into your media use through books, podcasts, Catholic radio, devotional apps, and Christian television.

Offer Clear Consequences

Children respond best when both rules and consequences are clearly laid out. When you discuss creating your family media rules, discuss the consequences that will occur if they misuse media. As parents, you may want to set these consequences yourself, but I encourage you to ask your children what they think are appropriate consequences before you set anything in stone. Children will offer you consequences that matter to them when you involve them in the discussion, and their involvement in creating their punishment will help them to stick with the rules you have agreed upon. Remember that you may need to customize the consequences based on the child—taking away Internet privileges may be a huge punishment for one child, while another may care more about having to stay home from after-school activities.

Social and Moral Consequences

In addition to family-based punishments for media misuse, be sure to explain to your children that there are social and moral consequences that come with media misuse as well. Your rules exist to protect your children from the moral consequence of committing sin, but they also exist to protect them from the risk of becoming addicted to media or falling prey to the predators who have made media their hunting ground. You do not need to frighten your children, but you do need to make them understand what is at risk.

CHAPTER 8

The Church and the New Media

The Church exists to help guide and mold us as individuals and to support us as we struggle against temptation and sin, just as the individual members of our family would.

Parents cannot and should not try to struggle through raising their children to be thoughtful consumers of media on their own. The Church must participate in the process, helping parents and guiding children.

This chapter discusses many ways that individual churches can help their parishioners in their efforts to raise children who maintain a discerning and selective use of media throughout their lives.

Church Leadership

Priests and bishops need to face the issue of media consumption head-on. Individual churches and dioceses should discuss and create comprehensive guides for how they can help families and parishioners to use media while maintaining and encouraging Catholic values.

Teach Media at Mass

One of the most important things priests can do to encourage the healthy use of media is to include homilies on media during mass. Talk about the concerns your parishioners have come to you with in regards to media, discuss morality quandaries on popular shows, encourage a sense of responsibility in consuming media, and otherwise engage your audience as you would with any other topic.

Additional Advice from Church Leaders

Priests and parents alike should remember that the Church has published a number of documents over the years that offer guidelines for media use, both pastorally and in the home. These, among others, include Communio et Progressio, Inter Mirifica, Aetatis Novae, and some of the Popes' letters on World Days of Communication.

Church Community

Support from the Church as a community will also help parents and families to raise their children to be devout Catholics with discerning media consumption.

Discussion Groups

One of the very best things a church can do to encourage a Catholic-positive media environment is to create media discussion groups which meet regularly. I recommend splitting these groups into parents and children, then further splitting both of those main groups into smaller ones based on the ages of the children in the family.

Parent groups should talk about what media works and doesn't work for their family. They can discuss media they recommend, warn against any media they found to offer a negative influence, and provide each other with strategies for how to handle media that brings up values that are at odds with Catholicism.

Youth groups should have guided media discussions with a faith-based lens. Parent volunteers or other teachers can offer topics each week, or if the students are old enough, they can offer suggestions for what they want to talk about. If a student suggests a topic that may seem out of scope, take the time to discuss it with them to learn what lessons in Catholic morality they see in making that suggestion. Sometimes, students can see morality in popular media that we may not be able to see ourselves.

Family Media Events

Another way that churches can help to engineer a positive, faith-based media environment is to host family-friendly media events. Churches can offer movie nights, book clubs, and TV hours. Multiple churches or dioceses can arrange larger events, like concerts and discussions with famous authors.

When arranging these events, it is important to remember that not all media, even if it is Catholic-friendly, is appropriate for all ages. Concerts, for example, may be too much for very young children, or teenagers may turn their noses up at a more kid-friendly movie. It is a good idea to have something going on for every age group when a family media event is happening so that the whole family can be involved. Offering day care for little ones during a concert or an alternative event for teens during a kids' film can make a notable difference in the attendance of families as a whole.

Offer Internet Training and Media Literacy Classes

Today's world almost requires its citizens to be digitally literate and media-savvy. Churches can help their parishioners to learn the necessary skills to navigate media and technology by offering Internet training and media literacy classes. These classes can teach the following:

- Basic skills, like how to access the Internet, how to use search engines to find information, how to use email, etc.

- How to recognize email and phone scams and avoid them

- How to recognize bias in media, including news media, and how to check for facts over opinion

- Social media for parents — given how often the social media landscape changes, it is important for parents to keep up with the technologies that their children are using

Classes like these can help children and adults alike to successfully interact with media and technology. While it is important that parents educate children on safe media practices to create a healthy media environment in their home, it is equally important that the local churches reinforce this message at all levels of ministry and provide support for the entire family.

Offering Internet training and media literacy classes is especially important for churches who have high populations of the elderly, the young, and recent immigrants. Each of these demographics will need help learning how to use technology and how to protect themselves while they are online.

Be a Media Presence

Modern publishing platforms have made it easy for anyone and everyone to make their voice heard online. The Church has taken advantage of this by creating social media accounts, websites, blogs, and video content, which it shares online. However, some priests and local churches have not done a particularly good job in creating and maintaining their online presence.

Local churches should use all available resources to communicate with their members, including interactive websites, apps, social media, and texting. For example, St. Philip the Apostle in Lewisville, Texas, a parish in the diocese of Fort Worth, reminds parishioners of adoration times and local pro-life event information via email and text messages. The same parish uses Facebook to post upcoming events, holy day reminders, and parish news. Their communications team posts blog entries regarding new parish construction and the importance of sacred art and architecture. In a similar fashion, the Our Lady of Sorrows Church in Birmingham, Alabama posts all liturgical activities on their

Facebook page. Parishioners also have a clear view of the Adoration chapel and the daily adorers from the parish website.

If you are short-handed, as many churches are, offer a social media internship to college students at your church. They can gain college credit and valuable job experience while knowing that they are directly benefitting a cause they are passionate about.

Jesus Christ, the Supreme Pastor, after whose example the ministers of the Church strive to model their own pastoral ministry, implored all the available resources, and spoke the language of the people in order to effectively spread his message. There is no doubt that if he walked the earth today, he would use Facebook, Twitter, MySpace, and YouTube, to speak directly to the people. With over 14 million followers on Twitter, Pope Francis is at the forefront of this belief! In fact, a study of political use of social networking showed that the Pope has more clout than any other world leader based on his re-tweet numbers.[84] In 140 characters, Pope Francis is spreading the Gospel message to the world and engaging relevant issues head on. He is meeting the people where they are.

The Pontifical Commission for Social Communication stated several years ago:

> "While he was on earth Christ revealed himself as the perfect communicator. Through his incarnation, he utterly identified himself with those who were to receive his communication, and he gave his message not only in words but in the whole manner of his life. He spoke from within, that is to say, from out of the press of his people. He preached the divine message without fear or compromise. He adjusted to his people's way of talking and to their patterns of thought. And he spoke out of the predicament of their time."[85]

---

84   Fowler, 2014
85   Pontifical Commission for the Means of Social Communication, 1971

Priests are thus challenged to proclaim the Gospel by employing the latest generation of audiovisual resources (images, videos, animated features, blogs, websites) which, alongside traditional means, can open up broad new vistas for dialogue, evangelization, and catechesis.[86] If the Church is to communicate as effectively as Christ, and carry on the apostolic duty of preaching, teaching, and converting, they must speak the language of the people. A missionary would not move to a foreign country and expect to inspire and convert the local people by speaking English. No! He would learn the language and customs; he would become a part of the local culture in order to truly communicate. So must, priests, youth ministers, church officials, administrators, and volunteers find ways to reach the local population using modern means of communications.

It is vital to meet the people where they are, and they are on Facebook, Twitter, YouTube, Instagram, and Snapchat. By becoming a media presence, churches can help in the pursuit of creating Catholic-friendly media, offer all parishioners another way to engage with their church on a daily basis, and reach new people across the local community and the world.

The Ongoing Importance of Evangelization

Jesus ordered His apostles: "Go therefore and make disciples of all the nations, baptizing them in the name of the Father and of the Son and of the Holy Spirit, and teaching them to obey everything that I have commanded you."[87] In this moment, Jesus commissioned the Church with spreading the faith to the corners of the earth, and nothing has changed in the millennia since.

This call to evangelization is crucial when we consider the relationship between the Church, Catholic families, and the media. Sharing media with Catholic-friendly values is wonderful—but there must be media produced with those Catholic-friendly values in order for us to share it with our children. Media can

---

86 Benedict XVI, 2010
87 Matthew 28:16-20

be used to encourage Catholic values in our children (and ourselves) and conversion in non-Catholics.

Every Catholic should take steps to encourage members of the media to produce content, which reflects Catholic values. The Decree of the Second Vatican Council on the instruments of social communications, Inter Mirifica, emphasized this calling: "It would be shameful if by their inactivity Catholics allowed the word of God to be silenced or obstructed by the technical difficulties which these media present and by their admittedly enormous cost […] For the main aim of all these is to propagate and defend the truth and to secure the permeation of society by Christian values."[88]

Ten years later, Pope Paul VI reiterated this belief: "The Church would feel guilty before the Lord if she did not utilize these powerful means that human skill is daily rendering more perfect" for evangelization.[89] Recently, the Church reminded us that "these media [are] 'gifts of God' which, in accordance with his providential design, unite men in brotherhood and so help them to cooperate with his plan for their salvation."[90] Advances in media are truly gifts from God, which we must use to further the Church's earthly mission.

Catholics should offer vocal, enthusiastic, and "effective support […] to good radio and television programs, above all those that are suitable for families. Catholic programs should be promoted, in which listeners and viewers can be brought to share in the life of the Church and learn religious truths. An effort should also be made, where it may be necessary, to set up Catholic stations. In such instances, however, care must be taken that their programs are outstanding for their standards of excellence and achievement."[91]

---

88 Inter Mirifica, 1963
89 Paul VI, 1975
90 Communio et Progressio, 1971
91 Inter Mirifica, 1963

CHAPTER 9

Thoughts on the Family of God

The Church is God's family.[92] I found this sentiment reflected beautifully in the Our Lady of Sorrows (OLS) church in Birmingham, Alabama, where I found a new family as a child of God. This parish community is unique in so many ways. Its family emphasis is fascinating, as many, many families are endeared to the parish. The spirituality of this community brings to mind the early Christian community where the members were united in mind and heart. Even when parishioners relocate, their allegiance and commitment to the parish is unflinching; some come a long way to attend Mass and other activities at OLS.

The Reverend Monsignor Martin Muller (who prefers to simply be called Father Muller) is the architect behind the family spirit that reigns at OLS. He was named pastor in 1989, and since then, the Christian community has grown in leaps and bounds. Six masses are celebrated every weekend, all of which are well attended, and two masses are celebrated daily, not counting funerals. Fr. Muller is a loving, dynamic, and caring priest. He knows his parishioners so well, and his parishioners know him, too. It is a relationship that perfectly fits the good shepherd gospel narrative: "I am the good shepherd. I know my own and my own know me, as the Father knows me and I know the Father. Because of this I give my life for my sheep. I have other sheep that are not of

---

92   1 Tim. 3:15

this fold. These I have to led as well, and they shall listen to my voice. Then there will be one flock since there is one shepherd."[93]

I came to realize that Fr. Muller is a household name in Homewood and beyond. Once I had some work to do with a Baptist Christian in Homewood. When I introduced myself as a priest from OLS, she immediately pulled out a copy of the OLS Sunday Bulletin and started telling me how much she loves Fr. Muller and his reflections "From the Pastor's Desk." I have also been to other places in Homewood where people, Catholics and non-Catholics alike, speak kind words about Fr. Muller.

Fr. Muller's presence as a father figure speaks eloquently of the family bond that reigns supreme in OLS. In order to foster, strengthen, and uphold the family values, church groups and ministries have been created. In the recent introduction to the 2016 Directory of OLS, Fr. Muller wrote:

> "It is our hope that this Information Directory gives each parishioner an overview of all ministries, programs, committees and organizations that make up the Our Lady of Sorrows parish family. We pray it helps you find your place in our parish community. It is meant to be informative and we pray that it is inspirational-for there are many people that make our parish wonderful through the variety of all the different opportunities. To summarize, OLS embodies the teachings of Christ and through the teachings of Christ we lead by example in the collection of groups throughout our parish, actively contributing our talents and gifts towards the Church."

Despite the challenges that families in the U.S. have to grapple with concerning the media, the OLS families are certainly on the right path, keeping traditional family values intact. The bond is remarkable as parents come to church together with their children. Speakers are invited now and then to address issues pertaining to the faith and family life. The children of many parishioners are

---

93   Jn. 10:14-16

enrolled in the OLS School. The school has teachers of exceptional dedication. All this goes a long way to strengthen the family spirituality that flows to the faith community and back to the families. During my visit to the many families, we spoke about media and family life, and it appeared that every effort was made to not let media activities overshadow family moments.

Traditional family values are still strongly upheld among Catholics in this area, also commonly known as the "Bible belt" due to its Christian heritage. When gay unions were legalized in the U.S., our community seemed to be the most distraught. There was sadness all over the place. I will always remember the reactions of many parishioners. It happened that the Sunday following the legalization was dedicated to missionary appeals at OLS. Consequently, a missionary spoke in the place of the homily. As I greeted parishioners after mass, almost everyone expressed how they had hoped to hear that declaration denounced from the pulpit.

The easiest way to destroy society is to target the family. The legalization of gay unions is both anti-life and anti-family. In any case, it didn't take long for the liturgical readings to avail the opportunity to speak about marriage and family life.

The Importance of Traditional Family Structure in Society

The traditional family structure, in which children are raised by both biological parents, a man and a woman, is the gold standard for raising children in society. In no way does this position, held by the Church for decades, minimize the best efforts that single parents and others make daily to raise their families. There is no perfect family; every family, no matter how stable, has little knots to untie from time to time. Nevertheless, several studies in social sciences lend credence to the view that intact biological families are still the ideal.

First, research abundantly shows that the traditional family structure confers benefits on children throughout their lifespans.

Children raised by married parents in intact families are more likely to attend college, are physically and emotionally healthier, are less likely to be physically or sexually abused, less likely to use drugs or alcohol and to commit delinquent behaviors, have a decreased risk of divorcing when they get married, are less likely to become pregnant or impregnate someone as a teenager, and are less likely to be raised in poverty.[94]

What is the connection between traditional family structure and these socioeconomic and psychological benefits? The connection lies in the transmission of knowledge and skills from parent to child. Children receive gender-specific support from having a mother and a father. Research shows that particular roles of mothers (e.g., to nurture) and fathers (e.g., to discipline), as well as complex, biologically rooted interactions, are important for the development of boys and girls.[95]

Growing up outside an intact marriage increases the chance that children themselves will divorce or become unwed parents.[96] Children of divorce experience lasting tension as a result of the increasing differences in their parents' values and ideas. At a young age, they must make mature decisions regarding their beliefs and values—decisions which, in healthy psychological development, should be postponed until later years. For this reason, research supports marriage even over divorces in which the parents agree to work together to raise their children in harmony. In one study, children of these so-called "good divorces" fared worse emotionally than children whose parents were in unhappy but "low-conflict" marriages.[97]

Finally, an extensive study carried out by Mark Regnerus considered nationally representative data of children from various family origins: intact biological families, late-divorced families, stepfamilies, single-parent families, adoptive families, families with a lesbian mother, families with a gay father, and

94   Wilcox, 2011
95   The Witherspoon Institute, 2008
96   The Witherspoon Institute, 2008; Wilcox, 2011
97   Marquardt, 2006

other family types (such as families with a deceased parent or other combinations). The conclusions of his studies suggest that children raised in a traditional family structure are more stable socially, emotionally, and mentally. The relational outcomes of the participants in his study also show physical stability and a high sense of security.[98]

Taken together, this data provides ample evidence for the benefits of the traditional family structure. Although single parents and others parenting in non-traditional families do their best to provide loving and stable environments for their children, research shows that there is no substitute for the traditional family. This position, which is in keeping with the values of the Church, also reflects the biological, social, and emotional realities we observe around us.

Further Reflection on Marriage

Marriage is a basic human and social institution. Though it is regulated by civil laws and Church laws, it did not originate from either the state or the Church, but from God. Marriage is God's idea. After having created the heavens, the earth, and the animals, the creation story was incomplete until God created man in his own image and likeness and blessed him with the gift of marriage and procreation. "God said it was not good for man to be alone. I will make him a suitable partner...when he brought a woman to the man, the man said, at last this is bone of my bones and flesh of my flesh. That is why a man leaves his father and mother and clings to his wife and the two of them become one flesh."[99]

Since God is the Author of marriage, the Bible is the only guide for a successful marriage. Can we ever operate a gadget without the instructions? So how can we have a successful marriage without abiding by the Biblical precepts on marriage? The Church didn't invent marriage laws, but she has the mandate to

---

98   Regnerus, 2012
99   Cf. Gen. 2:18ff

safeguard such a divine treasure bestowed upon mere mortals, by proclaiming the truth about marriage at all costs and at times.

Neither state nor Church can alter the basic meaning and structure of marriage. Marriage, as instituted by God, is a faithful, exclusive, lifelong union of a man and a woman joined in an intimate community of life and love. This definition is not subject to revision or modification by humans because it is not within our competence to do so. Men and women who enter into a marriage commit themselves completely to each other and to the wondrous responsibility of bringing children into the world and caring for them. The call to marriage is woven deeply into the human spirit. Man and woman are equal. They are created different from each other for the good of the other. This complementarity, including sexual difference, draws them together in a mutually loving union that should be always open to the procreation of children.[100]

Marriage can only be the union of a man and a woman and ought to remain defined as such in matters of law. In a manner unlike any other relationship, marriage makes a unique and irreplaceable contribution to the common good of society, especially through the procreation and education of children. The union of husband and wife becomes, over a lifetime, a great good for themselves, their family, their communities, and society. Marriage is a gift to be cherished and protected.

Christ reiterates the point on marriage when he says, "Have you not read that the Creator from the beginning made them male and female?...This is why a man leaves his father and mother and becomes attached to his wife, and the two shall become one flesh. They are no longer two, therefore, but one flesh. So then what God has united, human beings must not divide."[101]

Divorce is not part of God's original plan for marriage. In the Gospels, the Pharisees approached Jesus and asked, "Is it lawful for a man to divorce his wife?" Jesus throws back the question at

---

100   see Catechism of the Catholic Church, nos. 1602–1605
101   Matthew 19:4-6

them: "what did Moses command you?" Indeed, Moses permitted a husband to write a bill of divorce because of their hardness of heart. These Jewish customs allowed men to treat their wives as second class citizens; husbands divorced their wives for flimsy reasons. For example, a man could divorce his wife in the evening if he returned home and felt disgusted about dinner. If the divorced woman was ever found with another man, she was accused of adultery, and she was stoned to death. Moses permitted a bill of divorce to free women from this kind of oppression.

Despite this unfortunate practice, Christ reiterates the point on marriage when he says, "But from the beginning of creation, God made them male and female. For this reason, a man shall leave his father and mother and be joined to his wife, and the two shall become one flesh. So they are no longer two but one flesh. Therefore what God has joined, no human being must separate." He goes on to say, "Whoever divorces his wife and marries another commits adultery against her; and if she divorces her husband and marries another, she commits adultery."[102]

Therefore, marriage is the one and ONLY sacrament that is administered from above, by the power of the Holy Spirit. These words need no further interpretation: "What God has joined together let no man separate." Whenever I officiate at marriage ceremonies, I am only playing the role of an official witness of the Church; I am not the Minister. The couples and God Himself are the ministers.

Before getting into marriage, the couple must seriously consider what they are about to undertake. Someone once said, "A wedding ring is the smallest handcuffs ever to have been made, so think deeply, choose your prison mate carefully and sentence yourself wisely to avoid a prison break." With this in mind, we can meaningfully declare: "I take thee to be my lawful wedded wife, to have and to hold, from this day forward, for better for worse, in sickness and in the health, for richer, for poorer till death do us part."

---

102   Cf Mk 10:2ff

A Response to the Legalization of Same-Sex Marriage

Marriage in the United States has been deviating from the Christian definition for some time, and it is saddening to witness. This divorce and remarriage, in some degree, have been present since the nation's founding. Adultery is commonplace, and sexual relations outside of marriage are more popular than ever. To top it all off, the Supreme Court of the United States struck another blow to the sanctity of marriage by legalizing same-sex marriages.

In the wake of this unsettling ruling, I have found comfort in a joint statement organized by the Ethics and Religious Liberty Commission of the Southern Baptist Convention, which reads, "While we believe the Supreme Court has erred in its ruling, we pledge to stand steadfastly, faithfully witnessing to the biblical teaching that marriage is the chief cornerstone of society, designed to unite men, women, and children. We promise to proclaim and live this truth at all costs, with convictions that are communicated with kindness and love."[103]

The unsettling legalization of same-sex unions by the Supreme Court of the United States on June 26, 2015, marked a stormy turning point in the history of the American people, and for the Church, it was no less a thunderclap than the legalization of abortion in 1973. In the weekend following the declaration, clergy, lay preachers, and civil authorities of diverse faith communities spoke out loud and clear against the Court's decision as a grave error of judgment. Since then, some Christians have asked me what my reaction would be if I were approached by a gay couple for marriage preparation in the Church—given that this has been established as a nationwide civil right. Though their inquiry seemed simple enough, it was a cause for deeper reflection on my part: first, because the law stipulates that homosexual and heterosexual couples have equal rights, and second, because my interaction with people of homosexual orientation is a pastoral reality.

103   Ethics and Religious Liberty Commission of the Southern Baptist Convention, 2015

To clear up this difficult question, I fell back on the faculties granted me by the local ordinary of the diocese where I am exercising my ministry. The faculty permits me to prepare couples for marriage and to officiate at marriages, as required by canon law. It does not allow the same from me for ceremonies that do not fit canonical requirements.

Marriage, as instituted by God, is a faithful, exclusive, lifelong union of a man and a woman joined in an intimate community of life and love. They commit themselves completely to each other and to the wondrous responsibility of bringing children into the world and caring for them. The call to marriage is woven deeply into the human spirit. Man and woman are equal. They are created different from each other for the good of the other. This complementarity, including sexual difference, draws them together in a mutually loving union that should be always open to the procreation of children.[104]

In accordance with the above definition of marriage, and in keeping with my religious beliefs, I am not obliged, de jure, to either prepare people for or officiate at any form of union that falls short of the Catholic meaning of marriage. As is admitted in the majority Supreme Court opinion, "the First Amendment ensures that religious organizations and persons are given proper protection as they seek to teach the principles that are so fulfilling and so central to their lives and faiths, and to their own deep aspirations to continue the family structure they have long revered."

As logical as my position may be, a bone of contention remains. In his dissenting opinion, Justice Clarence Thomas remarked, "Religious liberty is about freedom of action in matters of religion generally, and the scope of that liberty is directly correlated to the civil restraints placed upon religious practice." Consider Christian-owned businesses such as event venues, wedding photographers, bakeries, and florists; they are expected to render their services to both homosexual and heterosexual

---

104   see *Catechism of the Catholic Church*, nos. 1602–1605

couples without discrimination—not just in day-to-day deal-
ings but also in marriage ceremonies. This was the case with the
gentle-hearted Barronelle Stutzman, a seventy-year-old flower-
shop owner who was sued by a regular customer on grounds of
discrimination because she politely refused to provide flowers
for his gay wedding due to her religious beliefs.[105]

The Supreme Court's ruling hinges on an expansive redefinition of marriage, in an attempt to degrade it to a mere abstract
political concept. Justice Thomas, again in his dissent, high-
lighted this conflict:

> "In our society, marriage is not simply a governmental insti-
> tution; it is a religious institution as well. Today's decision might
> change the former, but it cannot change the latter. It appears all
> but inevitable that the two will come into conflict, particularly
> as individuals and churches are confronted with demands to
> participate in and endorse civil marriages between same-sex
> couples.…The majority appears unmoved by that inevitability.
> It makes only a weak gesture toward religious liberty in a single
> paragraph.…And even that gesture indicates a misunderstand-
> ing of religious liberty in our Nation's tradition."

Given that this conflict is a reality now that can't be ignored,
another question that parishioners are asking is, "What do we do
now?" My response is to stand up for your faith, to trust in God,
to love one another, and above all, to fast and pray. We can hold
our truths to be self-evident, regardless of the laws of man, for we
follow the laws of a higher power, the Lord our God.

Stand Up for Your Faith

The solidarity expressed so far among Catholics, Evangelicals,
and other faith communities in decrying the Supreme Court's
ruling is eloquent testimony of their witnessing for the sanctity
of marriage. But this is just the beginning of a long and painful

---

105   Harkness, 2015

journey, which brings to mind one of the Church's hymns that is popular in my homeland of Cameroon: "Stand up, stand up for Jesus, ye soldiers of the cross. Lift high his royal banner. Ye must not suffer loss. From victory unto victory, his army ye shall be, till every foe is vanquished and Christ be Lord indeed." There is good reason to begin a "March for Marriage" every June 26! There is an African proverb that says, "When you pray, move your feet." This means we should combine prayer with action toward the cause of our demands.

Speaking at a worship service on Sunday, June 28, Chief Justice Roy Moore of Alabama's Supreme Court announced, "Welcome to the new world. It's just changed for you Christians. You are going to be persecuted according to the U.S. Supreme Court dissents."[106] The president of our own Catholic Bishops' Conference, Archbishop Joseph E. Kurtz, released a statement that included a call to courage and perseverance:

> "I encourage Catholics to move forward with faith, hope, and love: faith in the unchanging truth about marriage, rooted in the immutable nature of the human person and confirmed by divine revelation; hope that these truths will once again prevail in our society, not only by their logic, but by their great beauty and manifest service to the common good; and love for all our neighbors, even those who hate us or would punish us for our faith and moral convictions."[107]

In God We Trust

Paradoxically, this battle for same-sex marriage is a battle against God, but it is the same God whose blessings are implored again and again by political leaders when they say, "God bless America." Regardless of how the Supreme Court rules on same-sex marriage, abortion, immigration, or any other issues, God remains sovereign. The numerous attempts so far to erase Him

---

106   Gass, 2015
107   United States Conference of Catholic Bishops, 2015

from the public square have been futile. It is therefore no co-incidence that on the very Sunday following the legalization of gay unions, the opening prayer at Mass (as found in the Roman Missal) all over the world read: "O God, who through the grace of adoption chose us to be children of light, grant, we pray, that we may not be wrapped in the darkness of error, but always be seen to stand in the bright light of truth."

O yes! God is not dead, so there is no cause for alarm! His sovereignty is eminent:

> "Why do the nations conspire? Why do the people plot in vain? The kings of the earth brace themselves and the rulers together take their stand against the Lord and his anointed.... Now therefore, earn wisdom O kings; be warned, O rulers of the earth. Sere the Lord with fear and fall at his feet; lest he be angry and you perish when his anger suddenly fares. Blessed are all who take refuge in him."[108]

Love One Another

Though the initial reaction of outrage and panic were expressive of the gravity of the offence, we must transcend a hostile approach in order to maintain our Christian identity at this sobering time: "Love one another as I have loved you."[109] To nurse thoughts of anger or hate against the government and people who disagree with our religious and moral precepts in general is evil. I have come across young people from African countries where the mere thought of gay rights is an abomination, yet they now identify as gay themselves. I equally en-counter and serve the spiritual needs of American people who not only identify as homosexual but also speak out in favor of gay-marriage rights. These, too, are God's creatures, and after the example of the Good Shepherd, they deserve God's love and care. When I speak about the divine plan for men and women

---

108   Psalm 2
109   John 15:12

and the LGBTQ[110] community as a whole, I also listen carefully to what they have to say. Love is our mission, and the truth must be spoken with charity.

We should also not lose sight of our own sinfulness and our need for repentance. This is, in fact, the best time to address our own sins, as we mourn for the sins of the whole nation. American Baptist pastor Warren Wiersbe is quoted as saying, "Truth without love is brutality, and love without truth is hypocrisy," and I agree. One without the other is detrimental to all.

Fast and Pray

Prayer is by no means the least weapon in this warfare. In fact, fasting and prayer are more important than speeches and protests. There is no better time than now to heed Saint Paul's call: "Pray without ceasing,"[111] especially if we are to be engaging in discussions about gay marriage. It should be recalled that sodomy, sexual perversion, and immorality were the root cause of the destruction of Sodom and Gomorrah, and the antidote to sin is prayer and the sacraments. The present suffering of the Church in the United States is a painful wound inflicted on the entire body of Christ, and prayers for healing are warranted. While this intention should be constantly a part of the faithful's prayer in Churches across the globe, it should also become an integral part of family prayers.

Keep True to Your Faith

The United States is an interesting place to be a Catholic and a Christian these days. A 2015 Pew Research Center study found that, "The Christian share of the U.S. population is declining, while the number of U.S. adults who do not identify with any organized religion is growing."[112] The decline in Christian faith spans all generations of adults, but it particularly affects young

---

110   Lesbian, gay, bisexual, transgender, and queer
111   1 Thessalonians 5:16
112   http://www.pewforum.org/2015/05/12/americas-changing-religious-landscape/

adults. Despite these declining numbers, the same study found that the U.S. is "home to more Christians than any other country in the world"—though those numbers are fractured amongst different branches of the faith and are largely Protestant.

So why are young people, despite their statistically likely Christian upbringing, turning away from Christ and His followers? Why do we so often hear stories of children who were raised to be good Catholics moving away from their faith?

These questions have troubled my soul since I came to this country, and there is no doubt in my heart that the answer is more complicated than what I have laid out in this book. Still, there can be no question that the new media plays a significant role in eroding Catholic values in children.

God commands us to raise our children in a way that is pleasing to His sight, and the cost is great should we fail. It is of the utmost importance for us to do what is in our power to instill Catholic values in our children throughout their lives so that they may live forever in paradise in the next life!

I encourage Catholics to move forward with faith, hope, and love: faith in the unchanging truth about marriage, rooted in the immutable nature of the human person and confirmed by divine revelation. It is hoped that these truths will once again prevail in our society, not only by their logic but by their great beauty and manifest service to the common good; and love for all our neighbors, even those who hate us or would punish us for our faith and moral convictions.[113]

Remain True to Your Roots

As Africans, respect for traditional family values is deeply rooted in our culture and has become an integral part of our identity. Please, let us never forget our roots! Your parents, family, and friends have made enormous sacrifices on your behalf,

---

113   United States Conference of Catholic Bishops, "Supreme Court Decision on Marriage 'A Tragic Error,' Says President of Catholic Bishops' Conference," June 26, 2015. See tinyurl.com/orbfkvu

and we must honor those sacrifices by living lives that reflect the values our loved ones would wish us to have.

We must also remember our humble beginnings as we search for greener pastures here in the U.S. Green cards and citizenship may change our status, but they neither take away our identity nor change the color of our skin. That's why we should remain connected to home—our true family is there.

As one teaches children about how to use the media and how to be good Catholics, one should teach them to be good Africans as well. Pass along family's traditions in this new world. Stay in contact with your family and friends in Cameroon so that your children will understand their heritage and the deep love of family that no oceans can separate.

Pathways to Reconciliation

The Church plays a pivotal role in the evangelization of families, but the Church itself rests in an unreconciled state. With the dramatic changes in communication, society, and values that we see in the new millennium, a call to reconciliation within the Church is more urgent now than ever. We cannot preach reconciliation to the outside world when we are not reconciled ourselves. I offer in this epilogue a perspective on reconciliation that will help us, within our families and within the Church, achieve the harmony we need to expand the embrace of the Christian community.

Please, Sir, Two Are Fighting

When I was growing up in Cameroon, fights were common among my peers, both in the neighborhood and at school. The petty squabbles that became fights were often rooted in jealousy, gossip, unhealthy competition, and simple misunderstandings. My peers believed that fighting and overpowering an opponent proved their superiority. When fights would occur, the rest of the boys would take sides, each fanning the flames of the conflict. The side we picked was not based on the truth, but rather on our relationships with the parties involved in the fight. For example, if Peter and John were fighting, John's friend would support him because of their friendship. A friend could be someone who shared meals, lived in the same neighborhood, or was a sometimes partner in crime.

If any of us decided to report a fight to the head teacher, there was only one way to say it: "Please, sir, two are fighting." We learned and rehearsed this phrase because public school kids typically spoke very little English. (Either Pidgin English or the native language was their first language.) The teachers took these matters seriously. They would interrogate the two fighters with a whip in one hand. The teachers were not concerned about who was wrong or right; they were concerned with the disgrace of fighting and the violation of the school rules and regulations. They frequently shouted, "Is that why you are fighting?" They felt the fights were petty and not worth the punishment we would receive: equal strokes of the lash for each of the fighting parties. After they dealt out the lashes, the teachers would discuss with us why the fight was futile. Finally, the teachers required the fighters to embrace each other in front of the entire class.

Some of the fighters were quick to see the uselessness of fighting, and it did not take long for them to eventually become friends again. There were instances when you could see them the very next day in the dining hall sharing a plate of rice and beans. When I look back, I can only appreciate our primary school teachers who, though not experts in conflict resolution, instilled in us the spirit of reconciliation and taught us about virtues that matter in life, such as peace, justice, and forgiveness.

A Shattered World

We are living in tumultuous times; nations are torn apart by wars and violence; communities are torn apart by political disagreements; families are torn apart by the weakening of traditional values through social media. The Church and Christian communities are not making much of a difference. As John Paul II (1984) articulated:

> It is a world in which divisions are seen in the relationships between individuals and groups, and also at the level of larger groups: nations against nations and blocs of opposing

countries in a headlong quest for domination. At the root of this alienation it is not hard to discern conflicts which, instead of being resolved through dialogue, grow more acute in confrontation and opposition. This has left many communities in total division and persistent fighting. (no. 2)

Sadly, these same problems exist within the Church as well. Speaking about the scandal of conflicts and division within Christian communions, John Paul II (1984) added, "Over and above the divisions between the Christian communions that have afflicted her for centuries, the Church today is experiencing within herself sporadic divisions among her own members, divisions caused by differing views or options in the doctrinal and pastoral field" (no. 2).

Plagued by this widespread dissidence, it is hard to find peaceful solutions to conflicts. Predominantly caused by the pursuit for wealth, gain, power, dominion, and/or racial hatred, these conflicts have caused deep pain and division in communities. St. James wonders aloud: "Those conflicts and disputes among you, where do they come from? Do they not come from your cravings that are at war within you? You want something and do not have it; so you commit murder. And you covet something and cannot obtain it; so you engage in disputes and conflicts" (Jm 4:1-2). Pope Francis (2014), in *Evengelii Gaudium,* further discussed the issue:

> Spiritual worldliness leads some Christians to war with other Christians who stand in the way of their quest for power, prestige, pleasure and economic security. Some are even no longer content to live as part of the greater church community but stoke a spirit of exclusivity, creating an "inner circle." Instead of belonging to the whole church in all its rich variety, they belong to this or that group which thinks itself different or special. (no. 98)

99

The Human Condition

Sin is the root of division: beginning with original sin, which all of us bear from birth as an inheritance from our first parents, extending to the sin that each one of us commits when we abuse our own freedom. Consequently, no matter how disturbing these divisions may seem at first sight, it is only after careful examination that one can detect their root. "Ignorance of the fact that man has a wounded nature inclined to evil gives rise to serious errors in the areas of education, politics, social action and morals" (*Catechism of the Catholic Church*, 2nd ed., 407).

Conflicting situations always arise when distorted desires begin to take control of the human mind. Examples of this distortion can be seen throughout the Bible, beginning with the first brothers. Distorted desires fueled Cain's jealousy against his brother Abel. Years later, Saul became jealous of David because David received better compliments from the populace owing to his victory of the Philistines. Entire kingdoms succumbed to feelings of jealously and rage, as seen in the division between the Northern and Southern kingdom of Israel. The people allowed their disloyalty to God, tribal hatred, and jealousy to come between all of Israel and Judah (Cf. 1Kings 12).

These consequences of sin are the reasons for division and rupture not only within each person but also within the various circles of a person's life: in relation to the family, to the professional, and to the social environment, as can often be seen from experience. Look no farther than the city of Babel and its tower to see division born from sin (Gen 11:1-9). Intent on building what was to be at once a symbol and a source of unity, those people found themselves more scattered than before, divided in speech, divided among themselves, incapable of consensus and agreement.

They failed because they had created a work of their own hands, and had forgotten the action of the Lord. They had attended to the horizontal dimension of work and social life, forgetting the vertical dimension by which they would have been rooted in God, their creator and Lord, and would have been directed toward Him as the ultimate goal of their progress. Social media and other technological developments make it easy today to become distracted in our attentions to God.

Beyond the Fallen Nature

Despite sinful inclinations, humankind alone has received a divine mandate to constantly seek unity, love and peace, for the well-being of each individual and the continued development of society. This is the implication of the creation story in which man alone was created in the image and likeness of his Maker and endowed with the intellectual faculty. As Pope Francis (2015c) expresses in his Encyclical on "Care for our Common Home," "Authentic human development has a moral character. It presumes full respect for the human person, but it must also be concerned for the world around us [...]" (no. 5). In a way, the divine architect entrusted to man the responsibility to build society by caring for creation and the temporal goods. It is impossible to adequately accomplish these noble tasks where people are divided, taking up arms against each other.

History attests to the devastating effects of unresolved conflicts. These have produced no good for human civilization and communities. If the present generation cannot learn from history, then humankind will continue to repeat the mistakes of the past—to the detriment of human progress and development. It has been said, "Insanity is doing the same thing over and over again and expecting different results." When the inability or denial to resolve conflict degenerates to physical and verbal wars, and widens the gap between opposing camps, it leads to the destruction of human life, human resources, and stagnation in the social and economic life of a people.

In advocating for peace during WWII, Pope Saint Pius X said, "Everything is lost with war, nothing is lost with peace." Reiterating the same sentiments on the 100th anniversary of the outbreak of WWI, Pope Francis added an impassioned plea urging countries currently embroiled in conflict to find "the necessary strength and wisdom" to embrace peace, citing current warfare between Israelis and Palestinians, as well as in Iraq and in Ukraine (Vatican City [AP] 2014).

It is not always true that time heals all wounds. This is the case when no concrete attempts are being made to properly redress the conflict. In matters of conflict resolution, a stitch in time can save nine. The longer it takes, while the warring parties viciously ponder ways to destroy each other, the deeper the wounds of sin and division become, making a fertile ground for the devil. St. Paul meant this when he said, "Be angry but do not sin. Do not let the sun go down on your anger, and do not make room for the devil" (Eph 4:26–27). The devil is the father of all division, called "schisms," which have been ripping the Body of Christ apart one conflict at a time.

The Church, more than any other institution on earth, faces the real challenge to rise beyond the fallen nature, because of the daily acts of reconciliation in the Liturgy. The Eucharist, known to be the "source and summit" of the Christian life is about reconciliation with God and with one another; both are inseparable. This is expressed in the Penitential Rite ("Lord have mercy"), the Lord's Prayer, the "Lamb of God," and the "Sign of Peace." If these prayers are repeated daily, yet those who offer them are enemies to each other, they become empty devotions, and the words of the Prophet become true: "Because these people draw near with their mouths and honor me with their lips, while their hearts are far from me, and their worship of me is a human commandment learned by rote" (Is 29:13). If we honor God in speech, but not deed, wouldn't our hearts become like the festering lily in Shakespeare's sonnet? "For sweetest things turn sourest by their deeds; / Lilies that fester smell far worse than weeds" (Sonnet 94, lines 13–14).

In his Apostolic Exhortation, *The Joy of the Gospel*, Pope Francis (2014) expresses painful sentiments on this topic when he writes: "It always pains me greatly to discover how some

Christian communities, and even consecrated persons, can tolerate different forms of enmity, division, calumny, defamation, vendetta, jealousy and the desire to impose certain ideas at all costs, even to persecutions which appear as veritable witch hunts. Whom are we going to evangelize if this is the way we act?" (no. 100). Truly, who would choose to join a church full of conflict and division? We help no one but the devil when we create war among our own ranks.

Pathways to Reconciliation

Salvation is entirely the wonderful history of reconciliation in which God, as Father, in the blood and the cross of his Son-made-man, reconciles the world to himself and thus brings into being a new family of those who have been reconciled. St Paul speaks about Christ putting an end to enmity through his death on the cross (Eph 2:16). Amidst the rivalries that have rocked the Church and continue to do so in our times, not least of which is the contention regarding traditional marriage and family values, there is only one way to healing: reconciliation. Any other option short of this would be scandalous!

John Paull II (1984) is right:

> To the people of our time, so sensitive to the proof of concrete living witness, the church is called upon to give an example of reconciliation particularly within herself. And for this purpose we must all work to bring peace to people's minds, to reduce tensions, to overcome divisions and to heal wounds that may have been inflicted by brother on brother when the contrast of choices in the field of what is optional becomes acute; and on the contrary we must try to be united in what is essential for Christian faith and life, in accordance with the ancient maxim: In what is doubtful, freedom; in what is necessary, unity; in all things, charity. (no. 9)

103

In Christ's final prayerful call to his followers he asks his father for unity. He prayed, "I ask not only on behalf of these, but also on behalf of those who will believe in me through their word, that they may all be one. As you, Father, are in me and I am in you, may they also be in us, so that the world may believe that you have sent me" (Jn 17:20-21). He not only prayed that his immediate followers would be one, but also that those who would believe the words of the apostles would be one.

The starting point of this wholesome path is embedded in the popular hymn: "In Christ there is no East or West, in him no South or North, but one great fellowship of love throughout the whole wide earth" (Oxenham 1908). The hymn echoes the belief that the body of Christ—the Church—is one body, working in unison throughout the world; there is no place for division, only unity.

We Have All Sinned

We constantly need reconciliation because of our human sinfulness, which is the root of all evil and the cause for division. In the words of St. John the apostle, "If we say that we have no sin, we deceive ourselves, and the truth is not in us" (1 Jn 1:8). Conflicts usually lead to bitter exchanges whereby the parties insult, judge, and condemn each other. Whatever the cause(s) of the conflict may be, all parties become guilty before God and, until everyone is humble enough to acknowledge that guilt, there can be no pathway to reconciliation. John Paul II (1984) meant this when he said:

Reconciliation, therefore, in order to be complete necessarily requires liberation from sin, which is to be rejected in its deepest roots. Thus a close internal link unites conversion and reconciliation. It is impossible to split these two realities or to speak of one and say nothing of the other. The synod at the same time spoke about the reconciliation of the whole human family and of the conversion of the heart of every individual, of his or her return to God: It did so because it wished to recognize and proclaim the fact that there can be no union among people without

104

an internal change in each individual. Personal conversion is the necessary path to harmony between individuals (no. 4).

Truth and Charity

"Speak the truth and shame the devil!" is a telling saying. Truth is pivotal in every reconciliation process. Without truth, reconciliation is nothing more than sugarcoated words and a ticking time bomb. As Warren Wiersbe rightly said, "Truth without love is brutality, and love without truth is hypocrisy." Thus speaking the truth demands some considerable respect for the dignity of the human person. One without the other simply is not enough. In the Bull of Indiction on the Jubilee Year of Mercy, Pope Francis (2015b) recalls the essential spirit of Vatican II: "Errors were condemned, indeed, because charity demanded this no less than did truth, but for individuals themselves there was only admonition, respect and love. Instead of depressing diagnoses, encouraging remedies; instead of direful predictions, messages of trust issued from the Council to the present-day world" (no. 4). In the time of social media, it is easy to speak and to spread errors and untruths; we must use the power of new technologies to spread truth and to come together in liberation.

No doubt, the truth alone liberates; it is like a light shining in the darkness. Emeritus Pope Benedict XVI (2009) says, "Truth, by enabling men and women to let go of their subjective opinions and impressions, allows them to move beyond cultural and historical limitations and to come together in the assessment of the value and substance of things. Truth opens and unites our minds in the logos of love" (no. 4). Moreover, "Because it is a gift received by everyone, charity in truth is a force that builds community, it brings all people together without imposing barriers or limits. The human community that we build by ourselves can never, purely by its own strength, be a fully fraternal community, nor can it overcome every division and become a truly universal community" (no. 34).

Christ places charity above severity in the case of the woman caught in the act of adultery when he openly challenges the Jews. "Let the one among you who has not sinned be the first to cast a stone at her." When they had left one by one, he dismissed the woman saying, "Go and sin no more" (Jn 8:7,8). It is grossly uncharitable and ridiculous to publicize people's failings in any way. Whenever we face opponents with cruel truth, we make ourselves judge. Do not judge and you will not be judged because the judgement you give is the judgement you will receive (Lk 6:37).

Justice and Mercy

One of the great obstacles to reconciliation can be the human concept of justice that is limited to retribution. It would seem many, Christians included, still abide by the "*lex talionis*" rule—an eye for an eye and a tooth for a tooth. When property has been squandered, names sullied, relationships destroyed, and animosity has reached its peak, people can develop stiff necks and hardened hearts. Justice is a fundamental concept for civil society, which is meant to be governed by the rule of law. Justice is also understood as that which is rightly due to each individual.

No doubt, restitution can be an integral part of the reconciliation process, as well as a sign of conversion, as in the case of Zacchaeus, the tax collector, who resolved to pay back four times as much of all he has extorted (Lk 19:8). Retribution is usually the hallmark of judicial systems. However, though amends and restitution are equally important in the Christian process of reconciliation, the concept goes farther as beautifully expressed in Psalm 85:10: "Steadfast love and faithfulness will meet; righteousness and peace will kiss each other." In other words, reconciliation is still possible when the offender acknowledges his guilt, even though he lacks the means to pay for his offense.

St. James' admonition is meaningful: "Speak and act as those who are going to be judged by the law that gives freedom, because judgment without mercy will be shown to anyone who has not been merciful. Mercy triumphs over judgment" (2:12–13).

After all, as the Psalmist reminds us, "If you, O LORD, should mark iniquities, LORD, who could stand?" (Ps 130:3). Will there be a single person able to stand blameless before the judgment of Christ? Are we like the father or the brother in the story of the prodigal son? Surely, we should aim to be like the father who allowed his mercy to swallow justice. For, the loving kindness and mercy of the father irritated and enraged the oldest son; for him the happiness of the brother, who has been found again had a bitter taste (John Paul II 1984, no. 5–6). Avoid the bitter taste of the eldest brother by allowing God's mercy to temper human justice.

Mercy is not opposed to justice but rather expresses God's way of reaching out to the sinner, offering him a new chance to look at himself, convert, and believe. The experience of the prophet Hosea can help us see the way in which mercy surpasses justice. The era in which the prophet lived was one of the most dramatic in the history of the Jewish people. The kingdom was teetering on the edge of destruction; the people had not remained faithful to the covenant; they had wandered from God and lost the faith of their forefathers. According to human logic, it seems reasonable for God to think of rejecting an unfaithful people; they had not observed their pact with God and therefore deserved just punishment: in other words, exile. The prophet's words attest to this: "They shall return to the land of Egypt, and Assyria shall be their king, because they have refused to return to me" (Hos 11:5). And yet, after this invocation of justice, the prophet radically changes his speech and reveals the true face of God: "How can I give you up, Ephraim? How can I hand you over, O Israel? How can I make you like Admah? How can I treat you like Zeboiim? My heart recoils within me; my compassion grows warm and tender. I will not execute my fierce anger; I will not again destroy Ephraim; for I am God and no mortal, the Holy One in your midst, and I will not come in wrath" (11:8–9). God's anger lasts but a moment, his mercy endures forever.

In his Sunday Angelus Message of September 15, 2013, Pope Francis made very incisive remarks on the subject of God's justice as opposed to human justice: "The devil is shrewd, he deceives us with the idea that our human justice can save us and save the world. In reality, only the justice of God can save us! Jesus' sacrifice of his life on the cross is the supreme act of justice and is also precisely an act of mercy" (Lenartowick 2013).

On the Jubilee Year of Mercy

Pope Francis announced an historic event on April 11, 2015. For only the fourth time in Church history, there will be an extraordinary Jubilee year—the Jubilee Year of Mercy (December 8, 2015, through November 20, 2016). The Pope explains in the papal bull, *Misericordiae Vultus*, that Jesus Christ is the face of the Father's mercy. In this light, "Merciful like the Father" is the motto for the Jubilee Year. It comes from Luke 6:36, "Be merciful, just as your father is merciful." The Pope writes, "This is the time to heal wounds, a time not to be weary of meeting all of those who are waiting to see and to touch with their hands the signs of the closeness of God, a time to offer everyone the way of forgiveness and reconciliation" (Francis 2015a).

Without mercy, marriages end, communities separate, and friendships fall apart. We express this mercy concretely by forgiving one another as Christ forgives us. There is no limit to forgiveness, as Christ says, "Not seven times, but, I tell you, seventy-seven times," a number expressing limitlessness in Greek (Mtt 18:22). In the concluding instruction to the Lord's Prayer, it is clear and simple: "if you do not forgive others, neither will your Father forgive your trespasses" (Mtt 6:15).

A reconciled life is the new standard of Christian living. "So when you are offering your gift at the altar, if you remember that your brother or sister has something against you, leave your gift there before the altar and go; first be reconciled to your brother or sister, and then come and offer your gift" (Mtt 5:23–24). Even our sacrifices are not acceptable to God when we do not take the first step towards reconciliation.

True, it is not always easy to forgive and forget; especially when scars have been borne of serious conflict, particularly from loved ones. The Psalmist means this when he says if it were an enemy I could bear its taunts, but it is you my own friend, who ate from the same table with me who has stabbed me (Ps 55:12–14). Jesus Christ felt the same betrayal in the garden of Gethsemane when sweat came down his face like drops of blood, yet he surrendered his cup to his Father's will (Lk 22:39–46).

It is rightly said he who doesn't forgive others breaks the *bridge* over which he must *pass someday*. The fate of those who refuse to forgive as expressed in the Scriptures is doom. God expresses His wrath to the unforgiving servant who would not forgive his fellow debtor for a small debt, moments after being forgiven for a much larger debt. He squeezes the neck of his debtor. So God rebuked him saying, "You wicked slave! I forgave you all that debt because you pleaded with me. Should you not have had mercy on your fellow slave, as I had mercy on you?' And in anger his lord handed him over to be tortured until he would pay his entire debt. So my heavenly Father will also do to every one of you, if you do not forgive your brother or sister from your heart" (Mtt 18:32–35).

Mercy is not an option for Christians, because it is the core of the new commandment: "Love one another as I have loved you" (Jn 15:12). The commandment is a panacea encompassing the spiritual, social, and emotional well-being of the Christian. Lack of forgiveness can adversely affect our physical health, as research has shown. Physically, the body is in a state of stress. Muscles tighten, causing imbalances or pain in the neck, back, and limbs. Blood flow to the joints is restricted, making it more difficult for the blood to remove wastes from the tissues and reducing the supply of oxygen and nutrients to the cells (Luskin 2008). Lewis Smedes, author and theologian, rightly said, "To forgive is to set a prisoner free and discover that prisoner was you."

The Joy of Reconciliation

In certain African cultures, feasting is an integral part of reconciliation; no matter what it takes to bring families or communities together, it always culminates in some form of celebration. In several places in Scriptures, eternity is often depicted as a joyful banquet, as we see in Isaiah 55:1, "Ho, everyone who thirsts, come to the waters; and you that have no money, come, buy and eat! Come, buy wine and milk without money and without price." Every reconciliation ceremony is a time of great rejoicing, peace, and happiness.

Evidently, the human heart hungers more for eternal values like peace, justice, and reconciliation than for material food. There is hardly any true satisfaction where these values are absent, even if there is food in abundance. As expressed in the preface of the Solemnity of Christ the King, God's kingdom is a kingdom of truth and life; a kingdom of holiness and grace; a kingdom of justice, love, and peace (Cf. The Roman Missal). This is the kingdom that we repeatedly invoke in the Lord's Prayer, as revealed in the apocalypse of John: "They will hunger no more, and thirst no more; the sun will not strike them, nor any scorching heat; for the Lamb at the center of the throne will be their shepherd, and he will guide them to springs of the water of life, and God will wipe away every tear from their eyes" (Rev 7:16–17).

Emeritus Pope Benedict XVI (2009) said, "As a spiritual being, the human creature is defined through interpersonal relations. The more authentically he or she lives these relations, the more his or her own personal identity matures. It is not by isolation that man establishes his worth, but by placing himself in relation with others and with God" (no. 53). We are called to live authentic lives built on a foundation of charity, peace, and unity, without which our relationships become empty and fleeting.

Conclusion

The path to reconciliation is not frequently trodden in a world where pride, wealth, material gain, prosperity, and relativism have a firm grip on humanity. It takes humility and moral courage to take the first step towards reconciliation. These are not popular virtues. Alexander Pope (1709) is right: "To err is human, to forgive divine" (line 535). For genuine and lasting reconciliation to be attained, there is need for divine help. "The conviction that man is self-sufficient and can successfully eliminate the evil present in history by his own action alone has led him to confuse happiness and salvation with immanent forms of material prosperity and social action" (Benedict XVI 2009, no. 34).

Forgiveness and reconciliation are not the same thing. Forgiveness is a step towards reconciliation; it is the will and ability to let go of hurts and offenses. Where forgiveness is sincere, reconciliation follows. There is no better way to take this bold step of living a reconciled life than having recourse to the popular prayer of St Francis: "Lord, make me an instrument of your peace. Where there is hatred, let me sow love; where there is injury, pardon; where there is doubt, faith; where there is despair, hope; where there is darkness, light; where there is sadness, joy. O, Divine Master, grant that I may not so much seek to be consoled as to console; to be understood as to understand; to be loved as to love; for it is in giving that we receive; it is in pardoning that we are pardoned; it is in dying that we are born again to eternal life."

APPENDIX A

New Media and the Christian Family

Dear Student/parent

I am Rev. Wilfred Emeh, Associate Pastor at Our Lady of Sorrows Catholic Church, Birmingham, Alabama, and communication graduate major at UAB. I am currently carrying out a study on **New Media and the Christian Family.** The following questions are intended to provide me with the necessary data for the completion of my study. The first segment of questions (1 to 18) is designed for students only (5th to 12th grades); while the second part (questions 19 to 30) is designated to parents only. Rest assured that the information you provide here is strictly confidential, and it will serve ONLY the purpose for which it is intended. All questions are closed-ended, requiring that you simply tick your answer choice. If, however, your answer choice is "other," please explain the reason for your choice. It is not necessary for both parents in the same household to fill out the questionnaire. I would be very grateful if you could kindly attempt all questions in your section. Please, circle your answers.

SECTION ONE: FOR STUDENTS ONLY

1. *How frequently do you use the Internet?*
   a. At least twice a day
   b. Daily
   c. Two to three times a day
   d. Once a week
   e. Twice a week
   f. Never

2. *On the average, how much time do you spend online each time you log on to the Internet?*
   a. Less than 1 hour
   b. 1 to 2 hours
   c. 2 to 3 hours
   d. More than 3 hours

3. *What do you mostly use the Internet for?*
   a. Sending and reading email
   b. Using instant messaging
   c. Playing games
   d. Watching videos
   e. Research for school
   f. Reading websites (for news, sports, etc…)
   g. Other

3b. How often do you carry out the activity selected above?
   a. Frequently
   b. Occasionally
   c. Never
   d. Rarely
   e. No opinion

4. *Do you have a smartphone, iPod, or tablet (iPad) that you can use to access the Internet?*
   a. Yes
   b. No

5. *As you may know, there are social network sites like Facebook, MySpace, YouTube, Twitter, Hi 5, Instagram, etc. where people sometimes share their thoughts. How familiar are you with social network sites?*
   a. Very familiar
   b. Somewhat familiar
   c. Not sure
   d. Not too familiar
   e. Not at all familiar

6. *Which social network site do you use the most?*
   a. Facebook
   b. My Space
   c. YouTube
   d. Twitter
   e. Instagram
   f. Snapchat
   g. Other
   h. Do not use any

7. *Compared with other kids your age, how strict are your family's rules about using the Internet or social networking sites?*
   a. Very strict
   b. Stricter than most
   c. About the same as other families
   d. Not as strict as most
   e. Not strict at all
   f. Not sure

8. *About how many hours a day do you spend watching TV shows or movies at home?*
   _____ hours

9. *With whom do you watch TV shows or movies?*
   a. Mainly alone
   b. Mainly with my parents
   c. Mainly with my peers
   d. Mainly with my siblings
   e. Not sure

10. *How often do your parents monitor the programs you watch?*
    a. Frequently
    b. Occasionally
    c. Rarely
    d. Never
    e. Other

11. *How often do you and your parents discuss a show or movie you've watched or something you've seen on the Internet?*
    a. Frequently
    b. Occasionally
    c. Rarely
    d. Never
    e. Other

12. *Do you think any of the TV shows or movies you watch influence your understanding of marriage and family life?*
    a. Yes
    b. No
    c. Not sure

13. *People have different ideas about marriage. Which do you think is the right view of marriage?*
    a. Permanent union between one man and one woman till death do them part
    b. Union between one man and one woman, but open to divorce if necessary
    c. A union between any two adults who are in love; it doesn't matter if they are men or women
    d. Marriage is a burden and staying single is better
    e. Other

14. *If your church had a discussion group on your favorite social media site, would you join it?*
    a. Yes
    b. No
    c. Not sure

15. *How likely would you be to "friend" your priests or pastors on Facebook or follow them on Twitter, Instagram, or other social networking sites?*
    a. Very likely
    b. Likely
    c. Somewhat likely
    d. No opinion

16. *How often do you attend church services (such as Mass or other worship)?*
    a. More than once a week
    b. Almost every week
    c. Two to three times a month
    d. Monthly
    e. A few times a year
    f. Never

17. How old are you?
_____ years old

18. Which church denomination do you belong to?
    a. Catholic
    b. Protestant (Baptist, Methodist, Presbyterian, etc…)
    c. Non-denominational
    d. Pentecostal
    e. Other religion besides Christianity
    f. None

SECTION TWO: FOR PARENTS ONLY

19. *How often do you monitor your children's use of the media at home?*
    a. Frequently
    b. Occasionally
    c. Rarely
    d. Never
    e. Other

20. *How often do you watch TV or movies together with your children?*
    a. Frequently
    b. Occasionally
    c. Rarely
    d. Never
    e. Other

21. *How often do you discuss responsible media use with your children?*
    a. Frequently
    b. Occasionally
    c. Rarely
    d. Never
    e. Other

22. *Compared with other parents, how strict are your rules about how your children use the Internet or social networking sites?*
    a. Very strict
    b. Stricter than most
    c. About the same as other families
    d. Not as strict as most
    e. Not strict at all
    f. Not sure

23. *Which church denomination do you belong to?*
    a. Catholic
    b. Protestant (Baptist, Methodist, Presbyterian, etc...)
    c. Non-denominational
    d. Pentecostal
    e. Other religion besides Christianity
    f. None

24. *How often do you attend church services (such as Mass or other worship)?*
    a. More than once a week
    b. Almost every week
    c. Two to three times a month
    d. Monthly
    e. A few times a year
    f. Never

25. *How old are you?*
    a. 25–35 years
    b. 35–45 years.
    c. 45–55 years
    d. 55–65 years
    e. 65 years and above

26. *What is the highest degree you've completed?*
    a. High school diploma or GED
    b. Community college or Jr. college degree (2-year college)
    c. 4-year (Bachelor's degree)
    d. Graduate or professional degree
    e. No degree

27. *What is your gender?*
    a. Male
    b. Female

28. How many children are living in your household?

_____children

*29. Which of these **best** describes your parental status?*

    a. All my children live with both biological parents

    b. I am a single parent and all my biological children live with me

    b. All of my children are adopted

    c. Some of my children are adopted and some are biological

    d. I am a grandparent or other family member (uncle, aunt, etc…) serving as legal guardian to one or more related children

    e. I am step parent of one or more children in my household

    f. Other

*30. Which of these **best** describes your marital status?*

    a. Single, never married

    b. Single, divorced

    c. Single, widowed

    d. Married, first marriage

    e. Remarried, previously divorced

    f. Remarried, previously widowed

    g. Living with a partner, but unmarried

    h. Other

Presentation of Findings, U.S. Study

Table B1

Student responses to question 1: How frequently do you use the Internet?

No.	Rate of use	Frequency	Percent
1	More than once a day	105	57.7%
2	Daily	31	17.0%
3	Once a week	1	0.5%
4	Other (please specify)	8	4.4%
5	Two to three times a day	37	20.3%
6	Total	182	100.0%

Table B2

Student responses to question 2: On the average, how much time do you spend online each time you log on to the Internet?

No.	Length of use	Frequency	Percent
1	1 to 2 hours	54	29.7%
2	2 to 3 hours	17	9.3%
3	Less than 1 hour	81	44.5%
4	More than 3 hours	30	16.5%
5	Total	182	100.0%

Table B3

Student responses to question 3: What do you mostly use the Internet for?

No.	Purpose	Frequency	Percent
1	Watching videos	40	22.2%
2	Other (please specify)	32	17.8%
3	Research for school	22	12.2%
4	Sending and reading email	9	5.0%
5	Instant messaging	42	23.3%
6	Playing games	14	7.8%
7	Reading websites(for news, sports,etc)	21	11.7%
8	Total	180	100.0%

Table B4

Student responses to question 4: How often do you carry out the activity selected above?

No.	Rate of use	Frequency	Percent
1	Frequently	142	79.8%
2	Occasionally	32	18.0%
3	No opinion	2	1.1%
4	Rarely	2	1.1%
5	Total	178	100.0%

Table B5

Student responses to question 5: Do you have a smartphone, iPod, or tablet (iPad) that you can use to access the Internet?

No.	Ownership	Frequency	Percent
1	Yes	174	96.7%
2	No	6	3.3%
3	Total	180	100.0%

Table B6

Student responses to question 6: As you may know, there are social network sites like Facebook, MySpace, YouTube, Twitter, Hi 5, Instagram, etc. where people sometimes share their thoughts. How familiar are you with social network sites?

No.	Familiarity	Frequency	Percent
1	Not at all familiar	6	3.3%
2	Very familiar	135	74.2%
3	Somewhat familiar	34	18.7%
4	Not sure	1	0.5%
5	Not too familiar	6	3.3%
6	Total	182	100.0%

Table B7

Student responses to question 7: Which social network site do you use most?

No.	Site	Frequency	Percent
1	Instagram	83	46.1%
2	Twitter	12	6.7%
3	Snapchat	39	21.7%
4	Facebook	8	4.4%
5	Youtube	26	14.4%
6	Do not use any	12	6.7%
7	Total	180	100.0%

Table B8

Student responses to question 8: Compared with other kids your age, how strict are your family's rules about using the Internet or social networking sites?

No.	Strictness	Frequency	Percent
1	About the same as other families	63	34.6%
2	Not as strict as most	26	14.3%
3	Not strict at all	39	21.4%
4	Very strict	13	7.1%
5	Stricter than most	36	19.8%
6	Not sure	5	2.7%
7	Total	182	100.0%

Table B9

Student responses to question 10: With whom do you watch TV shows or movies?

No.	Watching method	Frequency	Percent
1	Mainly alone	84	46.4%
2	Mainly with siblings	36	19.9%
3	Mainly with my peers	12	6.6%
4	Mainly with my parents	38	21.0%
5	Not sure	11	6.1%
6	Total	181	100.0%

Table B10

Student responses to question 11: How often do your parents monitor the programs you watch?

No.	Monitoring level	Frequency	Percent
1	Frequently	26	14.5%
2	Occasionally	64	35.8%
3	Never	43	24.0%
4	Rarely	46	25.7%
5	Total	179	100.0%

Table B11

Student responses to question 12: How often do you and your parents discuss a show or movie you've watched or something you have seen on the Internet?

No.	Rate of discussion	Frequency	Percent
1	Frequently	36	19.9%
2	Occasionally	85	47.0%
3	Never	19	10.5%
4	Rarely	41	22.7%
5	Total	181	100.0%

Table B12

Student responses to question 13: Do you think any of the TV shows or movies you watch influence your understanding of marriage and family life?

No.	Opinion	Frequency	Percent
1	Yes	82	45.6%
2	No	63	35.0%
3	Not sure	35	19.4%
4	Total	180	100.0%

Table B13

Student responses to question 14: People have different ideas about marriage. Which do you think is the right view of marriage?

No.	View of marriage	Frequency	Percent
1	Permanent union between one man and one woman till death do them part	126	70.0%
2	Union between one man and one woman, but open to divorce if necessary	15	8.3%
3	Marriage is a burden and staying single is better	2	1.1%
4	A union between any two adults who are in love, it doesn't matter if they are men or women	32	17.8%
5	Other (please specify)	5	2.8%
6	Total	180	100.0%

Table B14

Student responses to question 15: If your church had a discussion group on your favorite social media site, would you join it?

No.	Decision	Frequency	Percent
1	Yes	72	40.0%
2	No	43	23.9%
3	Not sure	65	36.1%
4	Total	180	100.0%

Table B15
Student responses to question 16: How likely would you be to "friend"
your priests or pastors on Facebook or follow them on Twitter, Instagram, or other social networking sites?

No.	Likelihood	Frequency	Percent
1	Very likely	51	28.3%
2	Somewhat likely	51	28.3%
3	Likely	51	28.3%
4	No opinion	27	15.0%
5	Total	180	100.0%

Figure B1. Percentage of time spent online alone, or with parents,
peers, or siblings.

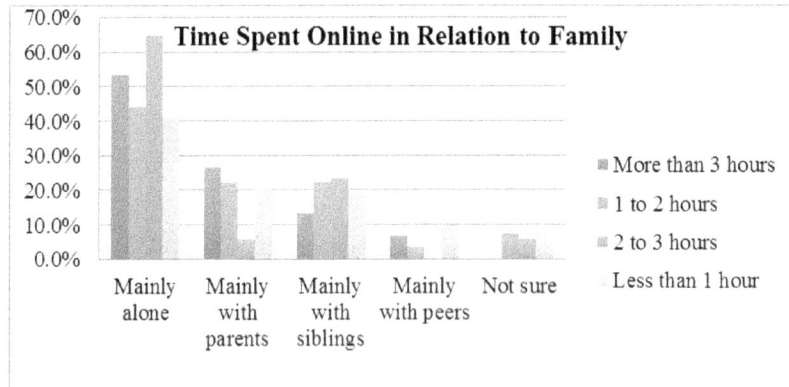

Figure B1 shows that the vast majority of children are mainly
alone when they are online. They spend their time instant messaging, chatting, playing video games, or multitasking. Of the
children who spend two to three hours online when they log on,
67.7% said they are mainly alone while online. Of these, only
5.9% watch movies or TV with their parents, and 23.5% do so
with their peers. The data shows that 53.3% of the children who
use the Internet for over three hours per day do so mainly alone.
Of these children, 26.7% watch movies or television with their

parents, and 13.3% do so with their siblings. The results show that 44.4% of the children who spend 1 to 2 hours each time they access the Internet are mainly alone. Of these children, 22.2% watch movies or TV with their parents, and 22.2% watch movies or TV with their siblings. The study also demonstrated that 40.7% of the children surveyed who spend less than one hour online do so mainly alone. Of these, 21% watch movies or TV with their parents, and 19.8% watch movies or TV with their siblings.

This figure demonstrates that when solitary Internet exposure reduces, time spent with other family members increases. Additionally, the percentage of children that watch movies with their peers is minimal.

Figure B2. Percentage of media exposure and perception of marriage.

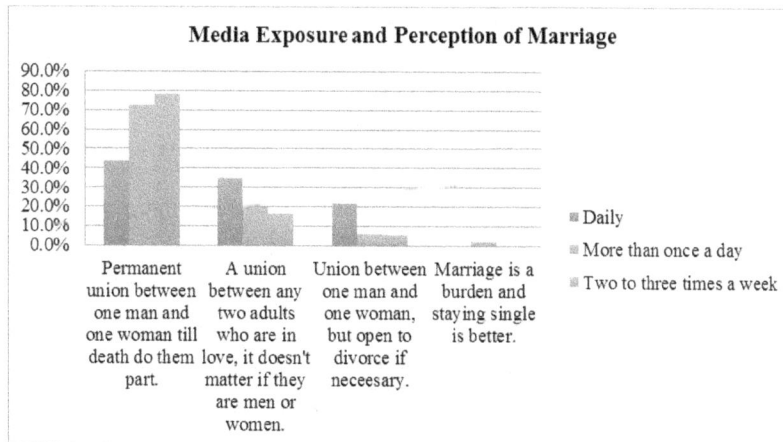

Figure B2 shows that the perception of marriage is determined by the level of media exposure. Of daily users, 43.8% uphold the traditional Christian view of marriage, while 34.4% are in favor of gay marriage. Among frequent users, 72.4% uphold the Christian view of marriage, 20% are in favor of gay marriage, and 5.7% are in favor of "marriage and divorce." Data analysis also revealed that 78.4% of children who are online two to three times a week are in favor of traditional Christian marriage, while

16.2% and 5.4% are in favor of gay marriage and "marriage and divorce," respectively. The results indicate that the higher the media exposure time, the more children's personal values deviate from the traditional Christian understanding of marriage. Even though $p > .05$, the outcome is worthy of consideration by the church and parents, given that over 70% of the kids represented in this study come from traditional Catholic homes.

Figure B3. Percentage of media exposure and views on marriage.

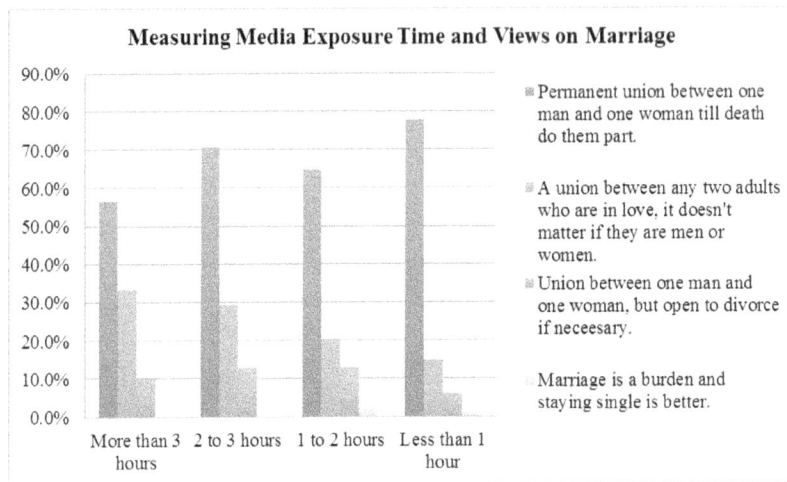

Figure B3 shows that 56.7% of children who spend more than three hours each time they log on to the Internet uphold the traditional view of marriage, while 33.3% and 10% of the same category accept gay marriage and divorce respectively. Of children who spend two to three hours online, 70.6% uphold the traditional views of marriage, while 29.7% and 13% are in favor of gay marriage and divorce respectively. Children who spend between one to two hours online uphold the traditional views of marriage 64.8%, while 20.4% and 13% are in favor of gay marriage and divorce respectively. Analysis shows that 77.8% of children who spend less than one hour online uphold the traditional view of marriage, while 14.8% and 6.2% are in favor of gay marriage and divorce respectively. The result reveals that the higher the exposure time, the more children are likely to deviate from the traditional view of marriage. This pattern is relevant though $p > .05$.

Figure B4. Percentage of parents' monitoring and views on marriage.

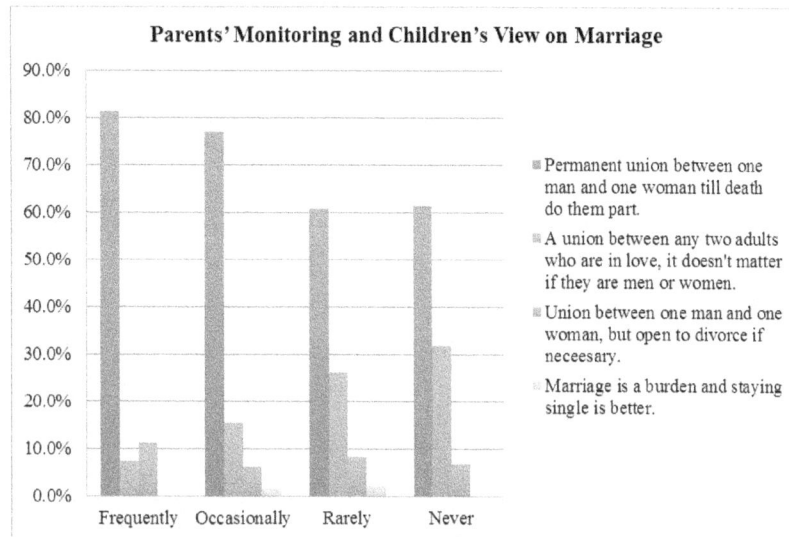

Figure B4 shows that 81.5% of children who are frequently monitored by their parents have a favorable view of traditional Christian marriage, while 7.4% and 11.1% are in favor of gay marriage and divorce respectively. Children who were monitored occasionally uphold the Christian view of marriage 61.4%, while 15.4% and 6.2% are in favor of gay marriage and divorce respectively. Additionally, 60.9% of children who are monitored rarely uphold the traditional view of marriage, while 26.1% and 8.2% are in favor of gay marriage and divorce respectively. Following the trend, 61.4% of children who are never monitored have a favorable view of Christian marriage, while 31.8% and 6.2% are in favor of gay marriage and divorce respectively. The results reveal that children who are regularly monitored are most likely to uphold the traditional Christian view of marriage, while children are most likely to favor gay marriage and divorce where monitoring is low or absent. This is indicative of how uncontrolled media exposure can shape children's beliefs and practices. The importance of this outcome cannot be overemphasized though $p > .05$.

Figure B5. Percentage representation of parents' involvement in media use and children's perception of marriage.

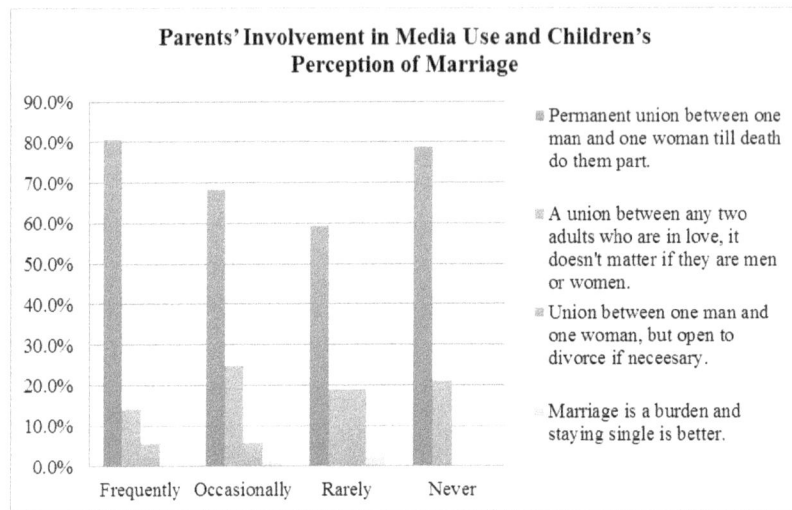

Figure B5 shows that 80.6% of children whose parents discuss media content with them uphold the Christian view of marriage, while 13.6% and 5.6% are in favor of gay marriage and divorce respectively. Of children whose parents occasionally discuss the media, 68.2% uphold the Christian view of marriage, while 24.7% and 5.9% are in favor of gay marriage and divorce respectively. The data also show that 59.5% of children whose parents rarely discuss the media with them uphold the Christian view of marriage, while 19% and 19% are in favor of gay marriage and divorce respectively. In a slight deviation from pattern, 78.9% of children whose parents never discuss media with them uphold the traditional view of marriage, while 21.1% of children

132

in the same category are in favor of gay marriage. This result indicates that the more parents discuss the media contents with their kids, the less they are likely to deviate from the traditional beliefs on marriage. On the other hand, when parents don't discuss the media contents, the children tend to be more in favor of gay marriage and divorce. The results regarding children whose parents never discuss media with them deviate from this expected pattern and may be worth further study. This outcome is important for the parents though $p > .05$.

Figure B6. Willingness of children to "friend" pastors or priests on Facebook or follow them on Twitter or Instagram.

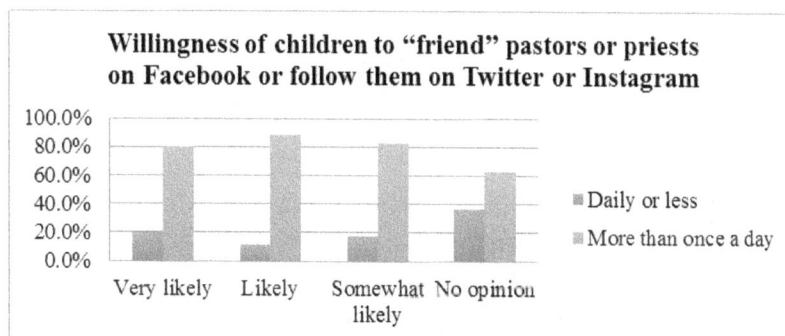

Figure B6 shows that 88.5% of children who are likely to engage with their priests or pastors on social networking sites are online more than once a day, while 80.4% who are very likely to follow their ministers on social media are online more than once a day. Among children who are online more than once a day, 82.4% of children are somewhat likely to follow their ministers, while 63% of the children who have no opinion on the subject are online more than once a day. Only 11.5% of less frequent users are likely to participate on social media platforms with their pastors, while 19.6% are very likely to do the same. Less frequent users identify as 17.6% somewhat likely to follow their pastors, while 37% have no opinion on their position ($p < .05$).

The results indicate that social media networking is an effective tool for evangelization for children who are online regularly. It is necessary for pastors and priests to be involved in social media to reach the vast majority of young people.

Table B16

Parent responses to question 1: How often do you monitor your children's use of the media at home?

No.	Rate of use	Frequency	Percent
1	Frequently	110	51.4%
2	Occasionally	85	39.7%
3	Rarely	14	6.5%
4	Never	3	1.4%
5	Other	2	0.9%
6	Total	214	100.0%

Table B17

Parent responses to question 2: How often do you watch TV or movies together with your children?

No.	Rate of use	Frequency	Percent
1	Frequently	105	49.1%
2	Occasionally	92	43.0%
3	Rarely	12	5.6%
4	Never	5	2.3%
5	Total	214	100.0%

Table B18

Responses to question 3: How often do you discuss responsible media use with your children?

No.	Rate of use	Frequency	Percent
1	Frequently	135	62.8%
2	Occasionally	74	34.4%
3	Rarely	6	2.8%
4	Total	215	100.0%

Table B19

Responses to question 4: Compared with other parents, how strict are your rules about how your children use the Internet or social networking sites?

No.	Strictness	Frequency	Percent
1	About the same as other families	70	32.6%
2	Not as strict as most	14	6.5%
3	Not strict at all	2	0.9%
4	Not sure	9	4.2%
5	Stricter than most	97	45.1%
6	Very strict	23	10.7%
7	Total	215	100.0%

APPENDIX C

Demographics of U.S. Study

Figure C1. Students' church attendance, U.S. study

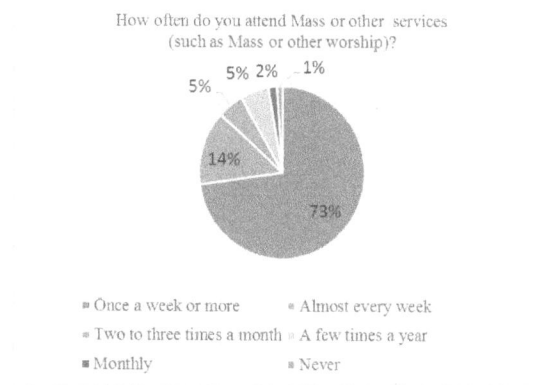

Figure C2. Students' age, U.S. study

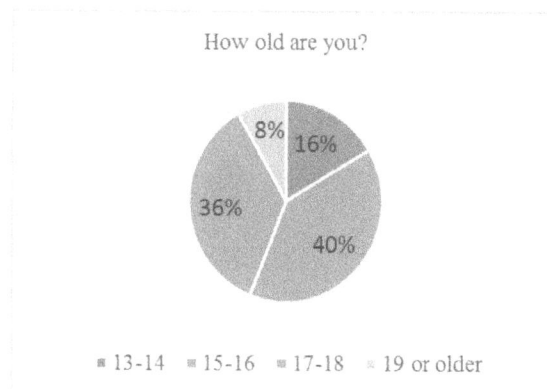

Figure C3 Students' denomination, U.S. study

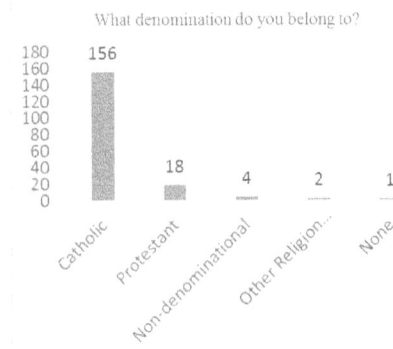

What denomination do you belong to?

Figure C4 Parents' denomination, U.S. study

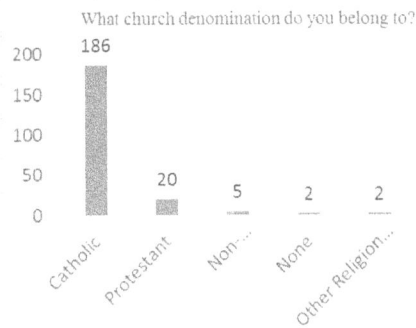

What church denomination do you belong to?

Figure C5 Parents' church attendance, U.S. study

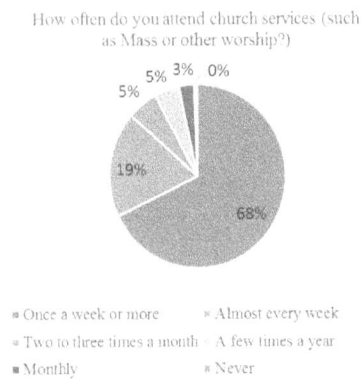

How often do you attend church services (such as Mass or other worship?)

- Once a week or more
- Almost every week
- Two to three times a month
- A few times a year
- Monthly
- Never

Figure C6 Parents' age, U.S. study

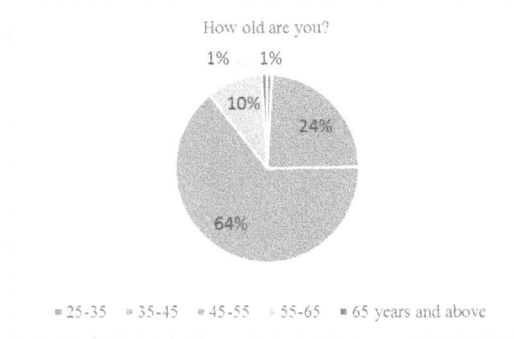

How old are you?

1%   1%
10%
24%
64%

■ 25-35 ■ 35-45 ■ 45-55 ■ 55-65 ■ 65 years and above

Figure C7 Parents' academic qualification, U.S. study

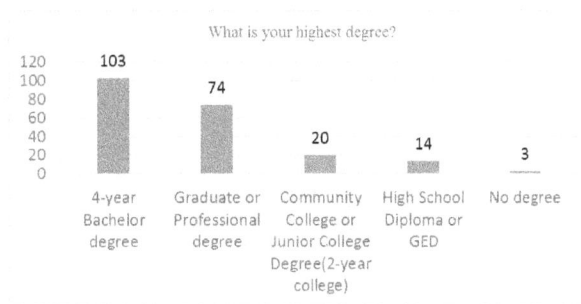

What is your highest degree?

103	74	20	14	3
4-year Bachelor degree	Graduate or Professional degree	Community College or Junior College Degree(2-year college)	High School Diploma or GED	No degree

Figure C8 Gender, U.S. Study

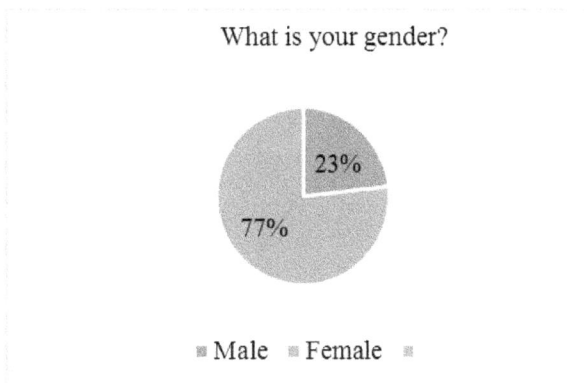

What is your gender?

23%
77%

■ Male ■ Female ■

Figure C9 Children in household, U.S. study

How many children are living in your household?

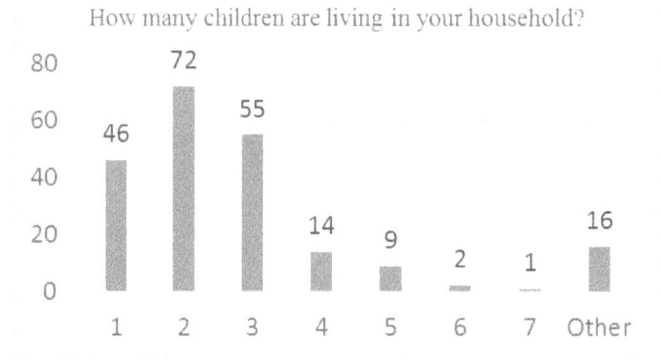

Figure C 10 Marital status, U.S. study

Which of these best describes your marital status?

Married, first marriage	171
Single, divorced	15
Remarried, previously divorced	14
Single, never married	6
Other	4
Single, widowed	3
Living with a partner, but unmarried	1
Remarried, previously widowed	1

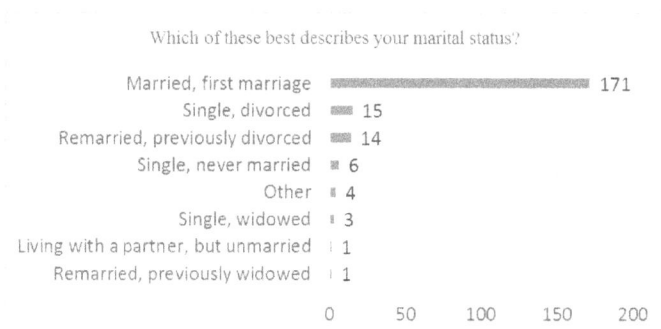

Figure C11 Parental status, U.S. study

Which of these best describes your parental status?

All my children live with both biological parents	171
I am a single parent and all my biological...	22
Other	9
All of my children are adopted	5
I am step parent of one or more children in...	3
I am a grandparent or other family...	3
Some of my children are adopted and some...	2

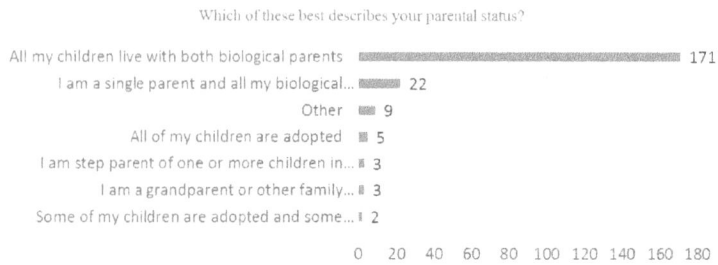

140

Presentation of Findings, Cameroon Study

Figure D1 Percentage of time spent online alone, or with parents, peers, or siblings.

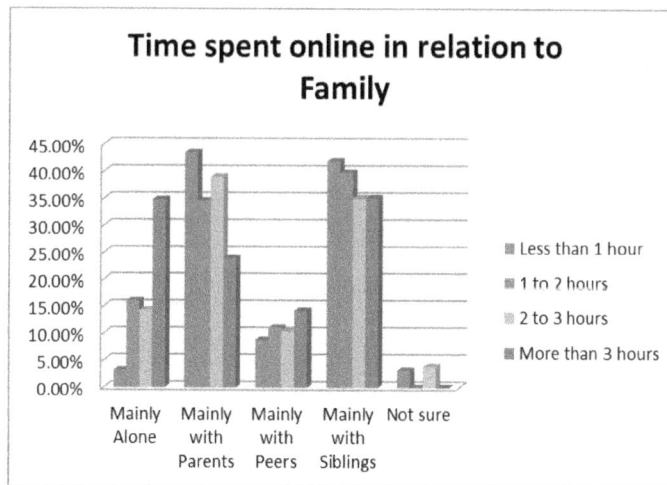

Figure D1 shows that a vast majority of children who spend less than an hour online, spend more time watching TV or movies with their parents and siblings. Of this category, 43.5% watch TV or movies with their parents while 41.9% watch TV with their siblings. Only 3.2% do solitary viewing. Of those who log on between one to two hours, 34.6% and 39.8% do watch movies with their parents and siblings respectively. 16% of the same category watch TV alone, while 11.1 % watch it with their peers. Of those who spend two to three hours online, 39% and 35.1% watch TV with their parents and siblings respectively. Only 14.3% and

10.5% do watch either alone or with peers. Of those who spend more than three hours online, 23.9% and 35.1% watch TV with their parents and siblings while 34.8% are engaged in solitary viewing and 14.2% do it with peers.

The representation of time allocation for online activities or Watching TV and movies with peers, parents and siblings or with self has an inverse relationship.

Figure D2 Percentage of media exposure and perception of marriage

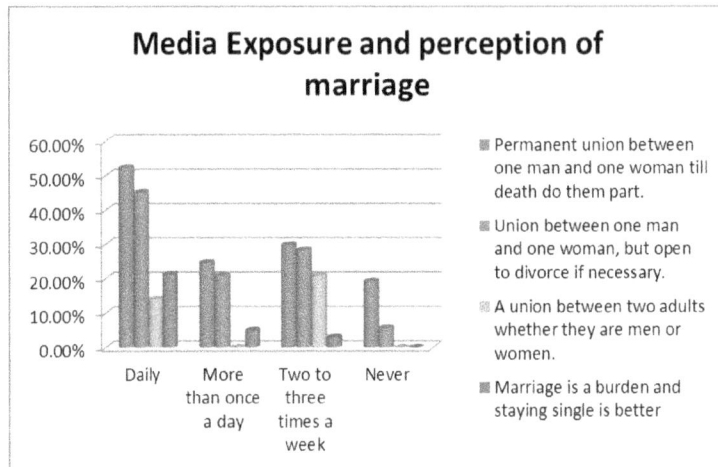

Figure D2 shows that the daily users of the Internet uphold the traditional views of marriage. Up to 54.4 % believe in the unbreakable bond of marriage, while 24.7% of the respondents who use the Internet more than once a day uphold the same view. Of those who use the Internet two to three times a week, 29.8% uphold the traditional view of marriage. And 19.2% of those who never use the Internet also believe in the Church's definition of marriage. 55.2 % of daily users think marriage should be open to divorce while 20.8 % of those who use the Internet more than once a day hold the same view. It is the same with 28.3 % of those who use the Internet two to three times a week, followed by 5.7% of non-Internet users. 14 % of daily users accept gay unions while 21% of two-three times users uphold gay unions. The table further shows that those who don't use the Internet at all are in line with traditional marriage except 5.7% that think that divorce should be an option.

Figure D3 Percentage of media exposure time and views on marriage

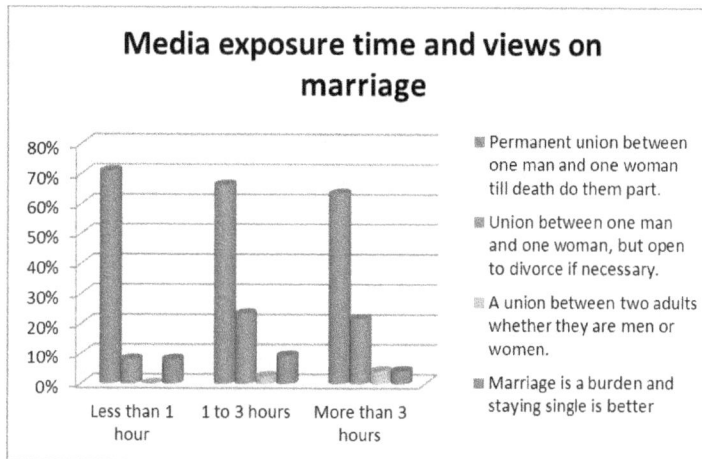

Figure D3 shows that 71% of children who spend less than an hour online each time they log on accept the traditional view of marriage, while 8.1% of the same category accept divorce. None of the respondents in this category accept gay unions while 8.1% consider marriage as a burden. Of those who spend one to three hours each time they log on, 66.4% uphold the traditional view of marriage while 23.4% have divorce as an option. Only 2.5% support gay unions while 9.4% consider marriage a burden with the preference to stay single. Of those who spend more than three hours each time they log on, 63.5% uphold the traditional view of marriage while 21.7% have divorce as an option. Only 4.3% are in favor of gay unions and the same percentage consider marriage a burden. The general trend here is that deviation from the traditional view of marriage is directly proportional to online time.

Figure D4 Percentage of parents' monitoring and views on marriage.

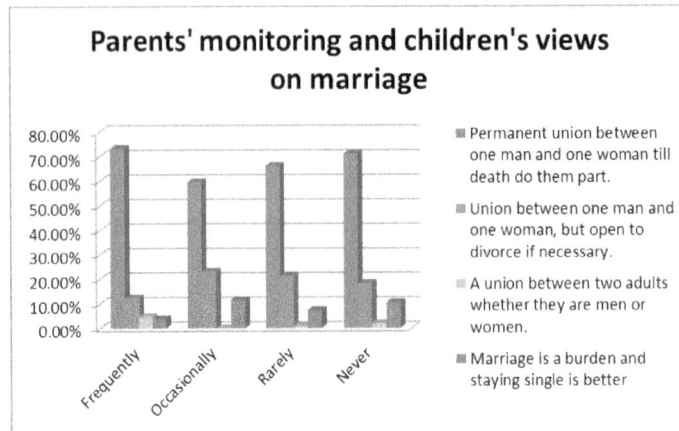

Figure D4 shows that 73.3% of those whose parents frequently monitor what they watch uphold the traditional view of marriage, while 12.4% accept divorce as an option. A minimal 4.8% and 3.8% accept gay unions and think of marriage as a burden respectively. Of those children who are occasionally monitored, 59.6% accept the traditional view of marriage while 23.1% consider divorce as an option. None accepts gay unions while 11.5% claim that marriage is a burden and staying single is better. Of those who are rarely monitored, 66.2% accept the traditional view of marriage while 21.3% have divorce as an option. Only 1.1 % are in favor of gay unions while 7.4% consider marriage as a burden. Of the children who are never monitored, 71.1 % uphold the traditional view of marriage while 18.4 % consider divorce as an option. Only 2.1 % accept gay unions while 10.5 % consider marriage as a burden. The bigger picture here is that children's viewership is naturally restricted to a family event in which monitoring is a given.

Figure D5 Percentage representation of parents' involvement in media use and children's perceptions of marriage

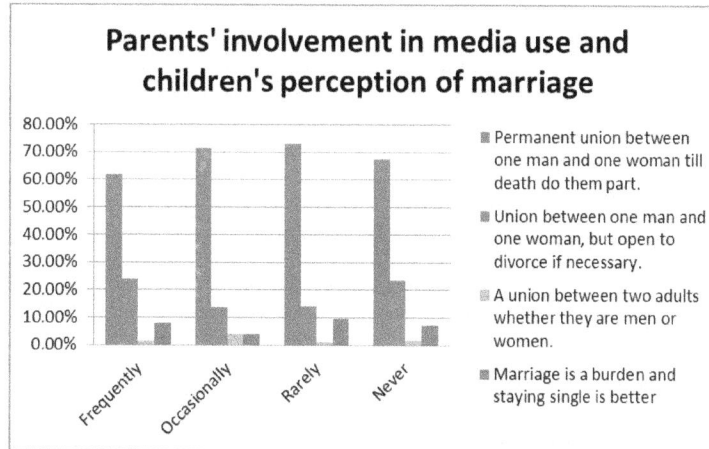

Figure D5 shows that 61.8 % of children whose parents discuss the media content accept the traditional view of marriage while 23.7 % consider divorce as an option. Only 1.3 % speak for gay unions while 7.9% think marriage is a burden respectively. Of children whose parents rarely discuss the media, 72.9 % are in favor of the traditional view of marriage while 14.1% consider divorce as an option. A minimal 1.2% and 9.4 % accept gay unions and consider marriage as a burden respectively. Of the children whose parents never discuss the media, 67.3 % are in favor of the traditional view of marriage while 23.6 % consider divorce as an option. Only 1.8% and 7.3 % are in favor of gay unions and think of marriage as a burden respectively.

Figure D6 Willingness of children to "friend" pastors or priests on Facebook or follow them on Twitter or Instagram

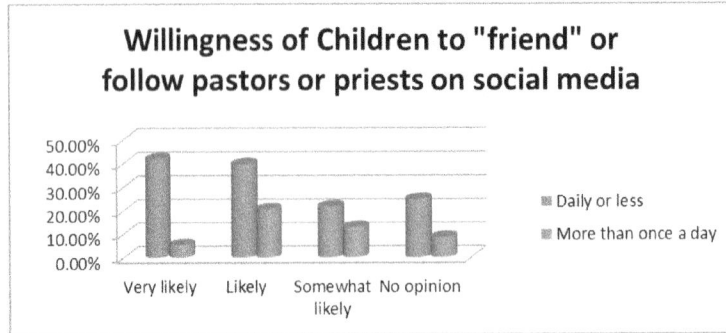

Figure D6 shows that 41.9 % of daily users and 5.4 % of respondents who use the Internet more than once a day are very likely to interact with the priest or pastor on social media respectively. Additionally, 39.7 % of children are likely to friend or follow their priest or pastor on social media while 20.6% of children who use the Internet more than once a day are likely to connect with their pastor on social media. Regarding those who are somewhat likely to friend or follow their pastor, the table shows 21.7 % of daily users and 13% of children who use the Internet more than once a day. Up to 24.8 % of daily users, and 8.6% of those who use the Internet more than once a day have no opinion on their position.

APPENDIX E

Additional Online Resources for Parents

The Catholic Church and Media

John Paul II, Message for World Communications Day, 1994
http://www.newadvent.org/library/docs_jp02tv.htm

John Paul II, *On the Role of the Christian Family in the Modern World*
http://www.vatican.va/holy_father/john_paul_ii/apost_exhortations/
documents/hf_jp-ii_exh_19811122_familiaris-consortio_en.html

Pope Francis, *Communicating the Family: A*
Place of Encounter with the Gift of Love
http://w2.vatican.va/content/francesco/en/messages/
communications/documents/papa-francesco_20150123_
messaggio-comunicazioni-sociali.html

Pontifical Council for the Family, *The Mass Media: A Gift and*
a Responsibility for All, a Commitment for the Families
http://www.vatican.va/roman_curia/pontifical_councils/family/
documents/rc_pc_family_doc_20080905_antonelli-media_en.html

Cell Phone Safety

National Crime Prevention Council
http://www.ncpc.org/topics/cell-phone-safety-1

OnGuard: Kids and Mobile Phones
http://www.onguardonline.gov/articles/0025-kids-and-mobile-phones

MyMobile Watchdog: Parental Controls
https://www.mymobilewatchdog.com

The United States Department of Justice Texting Safety
http://www.justice.gov/sites/default/files/
usao-id/legacy/2014/02/25/psctip.pdf

http://www.justice.gov/sites/default/files/usao-wdwa/
legacy/2012/08/18/tipsforparents.pdf

National PTA
http://www.pta.org/programs/content.cfm?ItemNumber=2153

Cyberbullying

United States Computer Emergency Readiness Team
https://www.us-cert.gov/ncas/tips/ST06-005

U.S. Department of Healthy & Human Services
http://www.stopbullying.gov

Educational Websites for Younger Children

PBS Kids Online Learning Tools
www.pbskids.org

Nick Jr. Learning Platforms
www.nickjr.com

National Geographic Kids
http://kids.nationalgeographic.com

Spatulatta Kids Cooking Tutorials
http://www.spatulatta.com

Brain Pop Online Learning by Subject
https://www.brainpop.com

Gaming

Entertainment Software Rating Board
http://www.esrb.org/about/inthegame.aspx

The Modern Parents Guide to Kids and Video Games
http://www.videogamesandkids.com

Focus on the Family: Parents' Guide to Video Games
http://www.videogamesandkids.com

CRC Health Group: Video Game Addiction
http://www.video-game-addiction.org

Internet Safety

National Crime Prevention Council
http://www.ncpc.org/topics/Internet-safety

The Federal Bureau of Investigation: A Parents Guide to Internet Safety
https://www.fbi.gov/stats-services/publications/parent-guide

Digital Trends: Free Parental Control Software
http://www.digitaltrends.com/computing/
best-free-parental-control-software/

Common Sense Media: Everything You Need
to Know About Parental Controls
https://www.commonsensemedia.org/blog/
everything-you-need-to-know-about-parental-controls

Media Plans

American Academy of Pediatrics
https://www.aap.org/en-us/about-the-aap/aap-press-room/
pages/managing-media-we-need-a-plan.aspx

American Academy of Pediatrics: healthychildren.org
https://www.healthychildren.org/English/family-life/Media/
Pages/How-to-Make-a-Family-Media-Use-Plan.aspx

Rules Agreement Contract
http://i.a.cnn.net/cnn/2007/images/03/22/online.agreement.pdf

Online Predators

National Center for Missing & Exploited Children
http://www.netsmartz.org/Parents

Covenant Eyes: Internet Accountability and Filtering
http://www.covenanteyes.com/2011/03/23/
Internet-predators-101-what-you-need-to-know-to-protect-your-kids/

The U.S. Department of Justice
https://www.nsopw.gov/?AspxAutoDetectCookieSupport=1

Pornography

Fight the New Drug
www.fightthenewdrug.org

HelpGuide.org
http://www.helpguide.org/articles/addiction/Internet-and-computer-addiction.htm#Internet_pornography

Focus on the Family
http://www.focusonthefamily.com/marriage/divorce-and-infidelity/pornography-and-virtual-infidelity/stages-of-porn-addiction

The Catholic Gentleman
http://www.catholicgentleman.net/2013/10/lets-talk-about-porn/

Extensive List of Catholic, Christian, and
Secular Resources for Porn Addiction
http://stthomasannarbor.org/anti-pornography-resources/

Social Networking Safety

McAfee: A Parent's Guide to Social Networking Sites
http://promos.mcafee.com/en-US/PDF/SocialNetworkinge-guide.pdf

Facebook Safety Center
https://www.facebook.com/safety

OnGuard Online: Protect Kids Online
http://www.onguardonline.gov/topics/protect-kids-online

Television Programming and Movie Rating Information

Parents Television Council
http://w2.parentstv.org/Main/

Common Sense Media
www.commonsensemedia.org

Parental Guide
www.parentalguide.org

Texting and Chatting Shorthand

NetLingo
http://www.netlingo.com/acronyms.php

NetLingo
http://www.netlingo.com/top50/acronyms-for-parents.php

DEFINITION OF TERMS

Catholic marriage: According to the Code of Canon Law, section 1, Catholic marriage is:

> ...the matrimonial covenant, by which a man and a woman establish between themselves a partnership of the whole of life and which is ordered by its nature to the good of the spouses and the procreation and education of offspring, has been raised by Christ the Lord to the dignity of a sacrament between the baptized. (Code of Canon Law, 1989)

Church: Church, as used in this work, refers to the Roman Catholic denomination, a Christian Church that traces its origin to Jesus Christ, with the Pope as its visible head, and known by its four marks: One, Holy, Catholic, and Apostolic (cf. McKenzie, 2015).

Media: Media refers to communication channels that spread news, entertainment, education, data, or promotional messages. Media includes every broadcasting and narrowcasting medium, including newspapers, magazines, television, radio, billboards, direct mail, telephone, fax, and Internet.

New media: New media is any form of media from 2000 onward to which a child could easily gain access. This includes material found on the Internet, including social media and other apps; television and movies, viewed through traditional means and through streaming services like Netflix, Amazon Prime, YouTube, Vimeo, etc.; print media, including newspapers, magazines, and books; and

153

music. The term generally implies that the user could access the material via desktop, laptop, and tablet computers or smartphones.

Social media: Social media are Internet-based applications that carry consumer-generated content, which encompasses "media impressions created by consumers, typically informed by relevant experience, and archived or shared online for easy access by other impressionable consumers" (Mangold & Faulds, 2009).

REFERENCES

A Preparatory Catechesis for the World Meeting of Families: Love is our mission: The family fully alive. Philadelphia, World Meeting of Families, 2015. https://www.worldmeeting2015. org/wp-content/uploads/2014/07/LoveisOurMission_final_ pdf.pdf

American Academy of Pediatrics. (2013, October 28). Managing Media: We Need a Plan. https://www.aap.org/en-us/about-the-aap/aap-press-room/pages/Managing-Media-We-Need-A-Plan.aspx

BBC News. (2015, June 16). Cameroon profile - media. http://www.bbc.com/news/world-africa-13146033

Benedict XVI. 2009. *Charity in Truth.* Vatican City: Libreria Editrice Vatican. http://w2.vatican.va/content/benedict-xvi/en/ encyclicals/documents/hf_ben-xvi_enc_20090629_caritas-in-veritate.html

Bennett, J. (2012, December 10). 'D' Is for 'Divorce': 'Sesame Street' Tackles Another Touchy Topic. *Time.* http://healthland. time.com/2012/12/10/d-is-for-divorce-sesame-street-tackles-another-touchy-topic/

Bryant, J., & Oliver, M. B. (Eds.). (2009). Media effects: Advances in theory and research. Routledge.

Bryner, J. (2010, March 9). Even a 3-Year-Old Understands the Power of Advertising. Live Science. http://www.livescience. com/6181-3-year-understands-power-advertising.html

Bumsub, J., & Seongjung, J. (2010). The impact of Korean television drama viewership on the social perceptions of single life and having fewer children in married life.

Asian Journal of Communication, 20(1), 17-32. doi: 10.1080/01292980903440806

Butterworth, G., & Nadel, J. (Eds.). (1999). Imitation in Infancy. Cambridge, UK: Cambridge University Press.

Catholic Church. (1997). *Catechism of the Catholic Church: Revised in Accordance with the Official Latin Text Promulgated by Pope John Paul II.* Vatican City: Libreria Editrice Vaticana.

Central Intelligence Agency. (2016, April 26). The World Factbook: Cameroon. https://www.cia.gov/library/publications/ the-world-factbook/geos/cm.html

Code of Canon Law: Latin-English Edition. Washington, DC: Canon Law Society of America, 1999.

Colford, S. W., Magiera, M., & Sloan, P. (1990). Athlete Endorsers Fouled by Slayings; Ads for High-Price Shoes Draw Criticism. *Advertising Age.*

Collins, R. L., Elliott, M. N., Berry, S. H., Kanouse, D. E., Kunkel, D., Hunter, S. B., & Miu, A. (2004). Watching sex on television predicts adolescent initiation of sexual behavior. Pediatrics, 114(3), e280-e289.

Committee on Public Education. (2001). Media Violence. *Pediatrics* 108 (5), 1222-1226; DOI: 10.1542/peds.108.5.1222

Common Sense Research. (2012, June 26). Social Media, Social Life: How Teens View Their Digital Lives. https://www.commonsensemedia.org/research/ social-media-social-life-how-teens-view-their-digital-lives

Communio et Progressio. (1971). http://www.vatican.va/ roman_curia/pontifical_councils/pccs/documents/ rc_pc_pccs_doc_23051971_communio_en.html

Ethics and Religious Liberty Commission of the Southern Baptist Convention. (2015) "Here We Stand: An Evangelical Declaration on Marriage." http://erlc.com/erlc/herewestand

Farrar, K., Kunkel, D., Biely, E., Eyal, K., Donnerstein, E., & Fandrich, R. (2003). Sexual messages during prime-time programming. Sexuality and Culture, 7(3), 7-37.

Federal Bureau of Investigation. (2011, May 17). Child Predators: The Online Threat Continues to Grow. https://www.fbi.gov/ news/stories/2011/may/predators_051711

File, T. & Ryan, C. (2014). Computer and Internet Use in the United States: 2013. United States Census Bureau. https://www. census.gov/history/pdf/2013computeruse.pdf

Francis. (2013). Meeting with the clergy, consecrated people, and members of diocesan pastoral councils: Address of Pope Francis. https://w2.vatican.va/content/ francesco/en/speeches/2013/october/documents/papa-francesco_20131004_clero-assisi.html

Francis. (2014). The Joy of the Gospel: Evangelii Gaudium. Vatican City: Libreria Editrice Vaticana. http://w2.vatican.va/ content/francesco/en/apost_exhortations/documents/papa-francesco_esortazione-ap_20131124_evangelii-gaudium. html.

Francis. (2015a). Homily on the Celebration of First Vespers of the Second Sunday of Easter or Divine Mercy Sunday. Vatican City: Libreria Editrice Vatican. https://w2.vatican. va/content/francesco/en/homilies/2015/documents/papa-francesco_20150411_omelia-vespri-divina-misericordia. html.

Francis. (2015b). Misericordiae Vultus. Vatican City: Libreria Editrice Vatican. https://w2.vatican.va/content/francesco/en/ apost_letters/documents/papa-francesco_bolla_20150411_ misericordiae-vultus.html.

Francis. (2015c). Laudato Si': On Care for Our Common Home. Vatican City: Libreria Editrice Vaticana. http://w2.vatican. va/content/francesco/en/encyclicals/documents/papa-francesco_20150524_enciclica-laudato-si.html.

Gass, N. (2015, June 29). "Roy Moore: Gay Marriage Ruling Will Lead to Persecution of Christians." *Politico*. tinyurl.com/ osr7tkn

Greenberg, B. S., & Hofschire, L. (2000). Sex on entertainment television. Media entertainment: The psychology of its appeal, 93-111.

Harkness, K. (2015, February 20). "State Says 70-year-old Flower Shop Owner Discriminated Against Gay Couple. Here's How She Responded." *Daily Signal.* tinyurl.com/oy7fmtk

Harvard Health Publications. (2010, October 1). Violent video games and young people - Harvard Health. http://www.health.harvard.edu/newsletter_article/ violent-video-games-and-young-people

Hoover, S. M., Clark, L. S., & Alters, D. F. (2004). Media, home, and family. Psychology Press.

Huesmann, L. R., & Taylor, L. D. (2006). The role of media violence in violent behavior. Annu. Rev. Public Health, 27, 393-415.

Impact of media use on children and youth. (2003). Paediatrics & Child Health, 8(5), 301–306. http://www.ncbi.nlm.nih.gov/ pmc/articles/PMC2792691/

Inter Mirifica. (1963). http://www.vatican.va/ roman_curia/pontifical_councils/pccs/documents/ rc_pc_pccs_doc_04121963_inter-mirifica_en.html

International Women's Health Coalition. (2016). Child, Early, and Forced Marriage in Cameroon: Research Findings. https:// iwhc.org/resources/child-early-and-forced-marriage-in- cameroon-research-findings/

Internet World Stats. (2014, March 31). Cameroon Internet and Facebook Usage, Population and Telecommunications Reports. http://Internetworldstats.com/af/cm.htm

Israelsen-Hartley, S. (2014, March 22). Parents are key to combating pornography, experts say. *Deseret News.* http://national. deseretnews.com/article/1224/parents-are-key-to- combating-pornography-experts-say.html

John Paul II. (1981) Apostolic Exhortation: Familiaris Consortio. http://w2.vatican.va/content/john-paul-ii/en/apost_ exhortations/documents/hf_jp-ii_exh_19811122_familiaris- consortio.html

John Paul II. (1984). Reconciliation and Penance. Vatican City: Libreria Editrice Vaticana. http://w2.vatican.va/content/john-paul-ii/en/apost_exhortations/documents/hf_jp-ii_exh_02121984_reconciliatio-et-paenitentia.html

John Paul II. (1990) Redemptoris Missio: On the permanent validity of the Church's missionary mandate. http://w2.vatican.va/content/john-paul-ii/en/encyclicals/documents/hf_jp-ii_enc_07121990_redemptoris-missio.html

John Paul II. (1995). Ecclesia in Africa: Apostolic exhortation. http://w2.vatican.va/content/john-paul-ii/en/apost_exhortations/documents/hf_jp-ii_exh_14091995_ecclesia-in-africa.html

John Paul II. (2004) Message of the Holy Father John Paul II for the 38th World Communications Day: The Media and the Family: A Risk and a Richness. http://w2.vatican.va/content/john-paul-ii/en/messages/communications/documents/hf_jp-ii_mes_20040124_world-communications-day.html

Kennedy, T. L., Smith, A., Wells, A. T., & Wellman, B. (2008). Networked families. Pew Internet & American Life Project, 1-44.

Lafraniere, S. (2005). Forced to marry before puberty, African girls pay lasting price. New York Times. http://www.nytimes.com/2005/11/27/world/africa/forced-to-marry-before-puberty-african-girls-pay-lasting-price.html?_r=0

Lancaster, H. (2015, June 3). Cameroon - Telecoms, Mobile and Broadband - Statistics and Analyses - BuddeComm. http://www.budde.com.au/Research/Cameroon-Telecoms-Mobile-and-Broadband-Statistics-and-Analyses.html?r=51

Lenartowick, K. (2013, Sep 15). "Forgiveness is the 'joy of God,' Pope says." *Catholic News Agency/EWTN News*. http://www.catholicnewsagency.com/news/forgiveness-is-the-joy-of-god-pope-says

Lenhart, A. (2015, April 09). Teens, Social Media & Technology Overview 2015. http://www.pewInternet.org/2015/04/09/teens-social-media-technology-2015/

Liu, J. (2015, June 26). Gay Marriage Around the World. Pew
    Research Center. http://www.pewforum.org/2015/06/26/
    gay-marriage-around-the-world-2013/

Livingstone, S., & Bovill, M. (2001). Families and the Internet: an
    observational study of children and young people's Internet
    use. http://eprints.lse.ac.uk/21164/1/Families_and_the_
    Internet_-_an_observational_study_of_children_and_
    young_people's_Internet_use.pdf

Lull, J. (1980). Family communication patterns and the social uses of
    television. Communication Research, 7(3), 319-333.

Luskin, F. 2008. *The Power of Forgiveness*. http://www.naturalnews.
    com/023304_forgiveness_body_health.html

Madge, C., Meek, J., Wellens, J., & Hooley, T. (2009). Facebook,
    social integration and informal learning at university: "It is
    more for socialising and talking to friends about work than
    for actually doing work." Learning, Media and Technology,
    34(2), 141-155.

Marquardt, E. (2006). *Between two worlds: The inner lives of children
    of divorce*. New York, NY: Harmony Books.

Miller, M. J. (Translated by), Christ's New Homeland-Africa:
    Contribution to the Synod on the Family by African Pastors.
    Ignatius Press, San Francisco, 2015.

Morgan, M., Shanahan, J., & Signorielli, N. (2009). Growing up with
    Television: cultivation processes. Media Effects: Advances in
    theory and research (pp. 34-49). New York, N.Y: Routledge.

New Revised Standard Version Catholic Edition. 1993. Washington
    D.C.: National Council of Churches.

O'Brien, J. (2008). Encyclopedia of Gender and Society, Volume 1.
    SAGE Publications.

Oxenham, J. (1908). In Christ There is No East or West.
    The Hymn Society. http://www.hymnary.org/text/
    in_christ_there_is_no_east_or_west_oxenh

Padilla-Walker, L. M., Coyne, S. M., & Fraser, A. M. (2012). Getting
    a High-Speed Family Connection: Associations Between

Family Media Use and Family Connection. Family Relations, 61(3), 426-440.

Paul VI. (1964). Dogmatic Constitution on the Church: Lumen Gentium. http://www.vatican.va/archive/ hist_councils/ii_vatican_council/documents/ vat-ii_const_19641121_lumen-gentium_en.html

Paul VI. (1975). Evangelii nuntiandi: Apostolic exhortation. http:// w2.vatican.va/content/paul-vi/en/apost_exhortations/ documents/hf_p-vi_exh_19751208_evangelii-nuntiandi.html

Perrin, A., & Duggan, M. (2015, June 26). Americans' Internet Access: 2000-2015. http://www.pewInternet.org/2015/06/26/ americans-Internet-access-2000-2015/

Pew Research Center. (2015, May 12). America's Changing Religious Landscape. http://www.pewforum.org/2015/05/12/ americas-changing-religious-landscape/

Pope, A. (1709). *An Essay on Criticism.*

Raising Children Network. (2015, June 16). Media benefits for children and teenagers. http://raisingchildren.net.au/articles/ media_benefits.html/context/1106

Regnerus, M. (2012). How different are the adult children of parents who have same-sex relationships? Findings from the New Family Structures Study. *Social Science Research, 41*(4), 752-770.

Rideout, V. J., Foehr, U. G., & Roberts, D. F. (2010). Generation M [superscript 2]: Media in the Lives of 8-to 18-Year-Olds. Henry J. Kaiser Family Foundation.

Roberts, D. F. (2000). Kids and media at the new millennium. Diane Publishing.

Rozenfeld, M. (2013). Television Romance and Real-Life Marriage. Scientific American Mind, 24(1), 10-10.

Schachman, K. A. (2010). Online fathering: The experience of first-time fatherhood in combat-deployed troops. Nursing research, 59(1), 11-17.

Shakespeare, W. Sonnet 94.

The Witherspoon Institute. (2008). *Marriage and the public good: Ten principles*. Princeton, NJ: Author.

United States Conference of Catholic Bishops. (2015, June 26). Supreme Court Decision on Marriage "A Tragic Error," Says President of Catholic Bishops' Conference. http://www.usccb.org/news/2015/15-103.cfm

US Department of State. (2008, March 11). Cameroon. Retrieved May 04, 2016, from http://www.state.gov/j/drl/rls/hrrpt/2007/100470.htm

Vandewater, E. A., Bickham, D. S., Lee, J. H., Cummings, H. M., Wartella, E. A., & Rideout, V. J. (2005). When the Television Is Always On Heavy Television Exposure and Young Children's Development. American Behavioral Scientist, 48(5), 562-577.

Vatican City (AP). (2014, Sep 28). Pope Francis Begs for an End to War on 100th Anniversary of WWI." *Huffington Post*. http://www.huffingtonpost.com/2014/07/28/pope-francis-war_n_5626976.html

Vitelli, R. (2013, July 22). Television, Commercials, and Your Child. Psychology Today. https://www.psychologytoday.com/blog/media-spotlight/201307/television-commercials-and-your-child

Wallace, K. (2014, October 7). The upside of selfies: Social media isn't all bad for kids. CNN. http://www.cnn.com/2013/11/21/living/social-media-positives-teens-parents/

Wikipedia. (2016, April 9). Fifteenth Amendment of the Constitution of Ireland. https://en.wikipedia.org/wiki/Fifteenth_Amendment_of_the_Constitution_of_Ireland

Wilcox, W. B. (2011). *Why marriage matters, third edition: Thirty conclusions from the social sciences*. West Chester, PA: Broadway Publications.

www.ingramcontent.com/pod-product-compliance
Lightning Source LLC
Chambersburg PA
CBHW050351100426
42739CB00015BB/3361